Good Cardinal Richard

ARCHBISHOP OF PARIS

by

Yvonne de la Vergne

Translated by

Rev. Newton Thompson, S.T.D.

B. Herder Book Co.

15 & 17 SOUTH BROADWAY, ST. LOUIS, MO.

AND

33 QUEEN SQUARE, LONDON, W. C.

1942

Contents

CHAPTER I

Boyhood

AT the very extremity of Brittany, on the confines of the Vendée and Maine-et-Loire, is a smiling countryside that used to be called the common Marches of Poitou and Brittany.

In early times it formed the frontier of Armorica. In the fifth century of our era it was under Roman domination and had often witnessed the conflicts between Caesar's armies, ambitious for new conquests, and the Celts, jealous of their independence.

Later St. Radegunda, the ruler of the district, brought it as her dowry to Clotaire, king of the Franks. Ever since the Church placed her on its altars, the parishes where she once ruled in this world have adopted her for their spiritual patron. Each year her feast is celebrated on the Sunday after the thirteenth of August. At Boussay especially, during the customary procession, the semi-

1

narians and the young men who have been called to the colors take pride in carrying her relics and her banners.

Under the rule of Blessed Frances d'Amboise, the Marches formed part of the countship of Nantes and became French, as did the old duchy, by Anne of Brittany's marriage to Charles VIII and to Louis XII. But these Marches enjoyed certain privileges and were exempt from the salt tax. The affairs of this little province were administered by a general syndic, and the assemblies continued to be held at Montaigu up to the Revolution of 1789.

This district of the common Marches of Poitou and Brittany is the place where we must look for the family origin of Cardinal Richard, Archbishop of Paris.

We find, in 1420, a certain Richard, notary at the manorial court of Tiffauges. In the sixteenth century the second son of Merry Richard, one Olivier, was a priest, doctor of laws, rector of Monnières, and canon of the cathedral of Nantes. In 1540 he was counselor at the "Parliament of the Great Days" which lasted from 1495 to 1554 and was replaced at that time by the Parliament of Brittany.

Later, René Richard married Marie, a lady of la Vergne. Since 1604 his family has borne the name

2

of the manorial estate where it finally became established. There Peter Richard de la Vergne was born. He became a priest, a doctor of laws, an advocate in the Parliament of Paris, and canon of the cathedral of Nantes. Thus he occupied a conspicuous place among the clergy of Nantes. On March 20, 1764, he was appointed pastor of Trinity Church at Clisson. Thus, after the lapse of a century, he took the place of an uncle of the same name, filling the same office. In his parish he founded a school, which occupied the site of the present city hall. His brother, Louis Richard de la Vergne, a member of the provincial Assembly of Poitou, was for twenty years a provincial magistrate and treasurer general of the common Marches of Poitou and Brittany. He shared the administration of this little province with the count of La Roche Saint-André and the marquis of Juigné.

In 1775 Canon Peter was delegated to petition Louis XVI for the confirmation of the privileges of the Marches and accomplished his mission so well that he was congratulated by the King.

In 1789 Peter Richard de la Vergne was chosen to represent his province at the States General. There he strove with all his energy for the royal cause and was one of the eight members named to bring about a union of the three estates. After the

3

October Days, he left the Assembly and returned to Brittany. But his refusal to take the oath to the Civil Constitution of the Clergy obliged him presently to go into hiding from the pursuit of the Revolutionists. He was seized on June 29, 1792, in the neighborhood of Clisson, brought to the prison of Nantes, proscribed, and deported to Spain. Upon his return to France after a long exile, he wrote to King Louis XVIII: "I had the consolation of finding my family still faithful. Everywhere I kept my unswerving loyalty to my bishop and to my king. . . . Providence has prolonged my days even to the age of eighty-eight years that I might witness the restoration of France with the return of His Majesty to the throne of his ancestors. Now I have nothing left to wish for and I can say with the holy prophet: 'Now Thou dost dismiss Thy servant, O Lord, according to Thy word, in peace; Because my eyes have seen Thy salvation.' "

When the Revolution broke out, the family house was inhabited by the oldest of the sons of Louis Richard de la Vergne, Louis Francis. At the height of the storm, he married Marie Genevieve Rosalie Poupart, daughter of Messire Charles John Baptist Poupart, chief officer at the Chambre des Comptes of Brittany, and of Marie Rose Gentet du Plessis. The young couple remained at Boussay and

4

by their influence sustained the courage of their countrymen. Then the insurgent force was organized to resist the Blues. On September 18, 1793, Kleber established his headquarters in a house that stands to this day on the square in front of the Boussay church. In the houses of the neighborhood scarcely anyone was left except the women, because the men had gone to Torfou to join the Catholic and royal army. Among them had gone Louis Francis Richard de la Vergne with his servants, leaving in the care of God his young wife and a little daughter only a few weeks old. The Blues marked their passage by murder, pillage, and incendiarism. As they left the town of Boussay, they invaded the la Vergne mansion; the young mistress of the house held her infant to her breast, seeking in this innocence a protection that would assure her the respect of the soldiers.

On the evening of that heroic day, which was a brilliant victory for the Vendeans, Kleber beat a retreat, passing again by Boussay. The last combats took place not far from la Vergne.

At the restoration of peace Louis Francis returned to his family. Several children were born, bringing joy to the home. They were: Marie Rose Magdalen, Charles, Louis, Joseph, Marie Rosalie; five other children who died almost immediately after birth; lastly Francis, born at Nantes, March 1, 1819.

Unfortunately again and again death entered the circle of this patriarchal family. The oldest son, Charles, lived only one year; five little angels merely entered into this world, only to leave it at once. Then, on June 4, 1818, Joseph was taken away at the age of twenty, just when he had finished his law studies at Paris. On this young man, so full of promise, rested the hope of the family; his parents, kneeling at his deathbed, could not hide their grief. The dying boy said to them gently: "Have courage. Next year I will have a brother to take my place with you. He will be your joy and comfort. Rejoice." In truth, the following year, on March 1, 1819, was born at Nantes, at number 15 rue des Etats, near the ducal château, the eleventh child: Francis, the future Archbishop of Paris. He was baptized the next day at the cathedral by Father de Trémeau, pastor and vicar general. For godmother he had his youngest sister, Marie Rosalie, and for godfather the husband of his oldest sister, M. René Benjamin Pellerin. M. Pellerin was the son of Joseph Michael Pellerin, deputy from Nantes to the States General, who had been one of the first gentlemen of Nantes to be arrested and imprisoned by the Revolutionary Tribunal.

6

The parents had scarcely begun to smile over their baby's crib, when their youngest daughter, Marie Rosalie, fifteen years old, took seriously ill and in a short time followed her brother Joseph to the grave. This gentle child died at la Vergne, July 18, 1819. At the time of her first Communion, she had asked her mother to give her a plain dress, so that the gift to the poor might thus be increased as a pledge of her happiness. Marie Rosalie did not long enjoy her godchild.

An older brother, Louis, had left home for the Seminary of St. Sulpice. On his way to Issy [1] the young Levite had stopped at Chartres to offer himself in a special manner to the Blessed Virgin and to consecrate his vocation to her. From his early boyhood, people noticed that Louis was conscientious even in the smallest matters. Later his keen mind, improved by serious study, remained hidden beneath a genuine humility. At Issy his conduct edified his fellow seminarians. M. Féret, the superior of the seminary at Nantes, says: "Louis Richard, at the end of his solitude, seemed no more to belong to earth." He was indeed ripe for heaven, and the divine Master would soon call him. His health declined rapidly. Unwilling to be exempted

[1] At Issy, near Paris, was located the so-called Solitude, where candidates for the Sulpician Society spent a year in spiritual preparation, corresponding to the novitiates of religious orders. Tr.

from any of the exercises of his retreat, he disregarded the medical advice and, when Doctor Récamier was called to his bedside, it was too late to check the disease. Our young Sulpician was not yet twenty-five years old when he died in the odor of sanctity at the Issy Solitude, October 3, 1820. We are told that, just before dying, the young deacon, speaking of his family and recalling the last words of his brother Joseph, said: "Tell my mother to be comforted. The son whom God has just given her will render signal service to the Church." The little Francis was then only seven months old.

Afflicted by these successive griefs, Monsieur and Madame Richard de la Vergne strove to cultivate in their last child the happy dispositions which they saw in him amid the native asperities of the Breton character. In this task they were aided by their oldest daughter, the big sister, married since 1816, who was like a second mother to her little brother. This big sister had her home at Nantes near her parents, who each spring returned to Boussay, taking with them their two grandsons, Louis and Charles Pellerin de la Vergne, the habitual companions of little Uncle Francis. Francis often went to church with his mother, but sometimes the devotions seemed a bit long to him, and he would ask in a whisper: "Mama, will you be through your

8

prayers soon?" The pious mother was disturbed at these dispositions in the boy and asked the prayers of the Carmelite nuns: "Pray for my Francis, that he may have a knowledge of the things of God."

At la Vergne the family had prayers and spiritual reading in common; each one in turn conducted the exercise. Once Francis, then five or six years old, made some mistake which caused the rest to laugh. At once he stopped and said: "People do not laugh when they are praying to the good God."

In his very early years, Francis did not have the gentleness of his brother Louis. His conduct became more and more unruly, and his parents attempted to moderate it by inviting the little boys of the town and of the tenants to play with him and his nephews. The old hedges used to resound with the shouts of the noisy children. At times they even had quarrels and fights. But nothing escaped Madame Richard's vigilance. She was always at hand to correct or reward as they deserved. This admirable mother took the same care of them as she did of her own.

On account of a pond that was in the garden, she was always a bit uneasy when the children were alone. At such times she stretched a cord at a certain distance from the house and made a rule that none of them should go beyond this frail boundary. But with special permission they sometimes raced their toy boats. Wooden sabots, those big sabots made out of beech wood, were lined up in the water; then each of the children, with mighty puffing and blowing, would try to send his boat beyond the others.

At meals, Francis and his nephews took without comment what was put before them, or had to be satisfied with dry bread. Sometimes Madame Richard would detect the children eyeing somewhat greedily a particularly delicious dish. Then, at the end of the meal, she would say: "Thanks be to God, you have all had enough to eat. We will take this to such and such a sick person." Perhaps the three young gentlemen would blush a little, but thus they learned to share with the poor.

Not far from Boussay, on the opposite bank of the Sevre, M. Richard owned the Echasserie estate. At that period no fine highway was available for the journey. The only way to go was on horseback over the steep hills and then to ford the stream and climb up the other bank. The children were too young to ride horseback by themselves, so they sat in two saddle-hampers. Louis, the oldest, was put in one hamper, with some stones as a counterweight; in the other were placed Charles and Francis. Francis, being a little heavier than Charles, used to bump against him at every jolt. Then Charles would complain: "Push over, push over; you are hurting me." But the prospect of playing with the bigger boys made up for the inconvenience of bruises and bumps.

Soon after reaching their playground, Louis and Francis were ready to fly their huge kite. As Charles got into the light wooden box fastened to it, he said: "I will take the risk." The experiment may, indeed, have been crude, but the contrivance would sometimes go as far as thirty feet to the great joy of the inventors, who did not then have any notion of air raids. In the excitement of their sport the children would go into the wet grass, and soon a call from M. Richard would moderate their enthusiasm: "Francis, come into the house at once, you have wet your feet; all of you come in." Madame Richard would dry her son's forehead and perhaps the boy would not perceive beneath the scolding the mother's anguish of heart. Even though the family spent a greater part of the year in the country, the health of this Benjamin remained delicate, and his parents had reason to fear that he might follow his older brothers and sisters to the grave. Francis could not be sent away to school, but at home, along with a serious education, he received an intellectual culture which developed

get the chocolate and divide it among you. If the ruffians come here again, I do not wish them to find any of it." These boys, even when they had reached a ripe old age, used to laugh at the recollection of this windfall of war.

Such was the environment in which little Francis grew up. With the years, his studies became more serious, and his zeal for the task became more sustained. Thursdays and Sundays were holidays from study. The young priests of the parish and the boys of the neighborhood usually came to take part in whatever pastimes were enjoyed on those days. When the noise of the outdoor sports reached beyond the walls of the park, the mothers used to smile and say to one another: "Monsieur Francis is stirring up our youngsters; but we need not worry when they are there." In fact, Francis had a lively good humor. Physical exercises were a restful recreation for him between the hours of study.

In 1834 a private school was opened for the girls of Boussay; the property was acquired by M. Richard in the name of his fifteen-year-old son. Francis took his post of proprietor seriously. Thereafter several children of the parish were in his charge in this establishment, and he offered his first baby's bed to start the furnishing of a little boarding school. When all French schools were secularized, this simple crib was returned to the family, where it is still kept as a sort of relic.

In 1836 the degree of Bachelor of Letters crowned our young man's studies at Rennes without thereby ending them. Intellectual labor always had a large part in his daily program, though it did not keep him from relishing the amusements and recreations of his age. He liked riding, took some pleasure in hunting, and was fond of long walks, which he took with rapid strides, probably carrying one of those pointed canes which the people of the Marches in earlier days used when walking along the stony roads. The distance between la Vergne and the little town of Clisson is about seven miles. One day, accompanied by a gamekeeper, he covered this distance in one hour and later on often referred to that record.

For young Francis life presented its happiest side. Endowed with the finest qualities, he always brought delight to those at his own home and to those of the neighborhood. He had the same affability in all his social relations and in his dealings with the tenant farmers of his family and with the poor people of the vicinity. When he went out for a carriage ride, his journey often concealed some charitable purpose. En route he prudently distributed his alms. Sometimes his purse was emp-

15

tied too quickly. One day his comfortable carriage robe was not with him when he returned from a ride to Clisson, "because," he confessed to his mother, "he had met someone who was cold."

His parents placed their hopes in this boy who took the place of their other sons that had died in infancy or youth. He gave promise of continuing the family traditions in a worthy manner. But on November 13, 1839, M. Richard was snatched from the affection of his family.

During the nineteen years since the death of his son Louis, M. Richard had the habit of reciting the breviary every day. On this day he had finished reading that day's office, and was suffering from a simple cold, when he was suddenly stricken with an attack. Francis, who with his mother was near M. Richard, ran for a priest. The curate at the Boussay parish was able to administer the last sacraments to the venerable dying man, who was unable to speak but who preserved his full consciousness. Less than an hour after the first alarm, Louis Francis Richard de la Vergne rendered his soul to God. That evening the following line was written in the family register: "His death was that of the just and leaves behind only regrets."

Thus Francis, at twenty years of age, found himself the head of the family. While accepting the prerogatives of that position, he intended especially to assume its duties. He possessed all the qualities of maturity and surrounded his mother with an affection that grew more tender and devoted each day. He endeavored to relieve her of every care and to second all her charities. With admirable prudence he looked after the management of his properties and continued at la Vergne a life filled with piety, labor, and humility.

Toward his brother-in-law and his oldest sister he remained full of consideration. Although he now asumed the title of uncle toward his nephews, he made no change in the brotherly affection which he showed them. Nor did he alter his charming relations with his own family. The loftiness of his character and the qualities of his mind made him always welcome in the social circles of Nantes. His talents, his fortune, the high standing of his family, and the esteem in which it was held made any career open to him. But his heart aspired to a greater perfection and cherished projects which at that time were known only to his spiritual director, Canon Courson, and Bishop de Hercé of Nantes.

The Trappist monastery of Meilleraye attracted the young man. He used to go there to find "fortifying examples of a laborious and penitent life."

The life of the cloister corresponded perhaps to his generous aspirations. Bishop de Hercé, however, said to him: "God has not given you an iron constitution, and the seminary will be better suited to you than the Trappist regime at Meilleraye." Divine Providence had its designs, and Francis' lack of a robust constitution kept him for the secular clergy. When the hour came to settle the question, Canon de Courson, a frequent guest at la Vergne, asked for an interview with Francis' mother. "Madame," he said, "I come to ask Francis from you." The poor mother had a presentiment of the sacrifice, yet her heart sank under the new trial: Francis would go away. She would no longer enjoy his presence. Among her many children, she would not have a son to continue the family. But the lively faith of this Christian woman promptly surmounted her suffering. She did not dispute the will of God, but at the foot of her crucifix sought the strength to pronounce her fiat and said simply: "He belongs to Thee, my God, before belonging to me." Then she recovered her habitual self-denial and seconded her boy's pious wishes, who continued for a while there with her his preparations for the priesthood.

Before his departure, the young man wished to regulate his temporal affairs in detail. To assure through his nephews the continuance of the traditions in the family home, he made an exchange of ownership with his sister, taking for his part the Echasserie estate, and turning over to her his rights to la Vergne. The nephews legally took their uncle's place, but Francis throughout his life remained the beloved and respected head of the family.

Not without some anguish Francis left his excellent mother, a most affectionate family, and the home of his childhood. His sacrifice and that of his family were shared by the entire household. A devoted servant, moved at seeing his young master departing, helped him in preparing his baggage and sadly handed him a pair of silver spurs which he was very fond of. Francis, with a kindly smile and with that graciousness which was always a mark of his personality, said: "I should indeed like to take them; but do you take them, my good Esprit; I will not wear them any more."

On October 19, 1841, after a journey of several days, Francis Richard entered the Seminary of St. Sulpice at Paris, and put on the cassock on All Saints Day.

CHAPTER II

Ordination

BEFORE leaving home, Francis had not been a student in any ecclesiastical house of studies; his mental and moral training was, however, judged sufficient for him to begin his theology at once. The three years that he would pass at St. Sulpice were filled with incessant work, sustained by a fine piety. His humble bearing veiled from the eyes of most of his fellow students the remarkable qualities which the superiors were able to appreciate. Often the young seminarian used to visit the Issy cemetery and kneel at the grave of his brother Louis. Then, strengthened by the edifying memory of that brother, he continued to advance along the way of perfection. Notwithstanding his spirit of recollection and his labors, Francis' thoughts every day flew to Nantes or Boussay, there to find those he cherished so fondly. The correspondence between him and his family enabled the family to share his new life, as it also continued to keep up his interest in the smallest details of theirs. His beloved mother was particularly the object of his solicitude. He had left her only to answer the call of God. And he was concerned that she should not be left too much alone at la Vergne, or during the winter in her house at Nantes. To his nieces he wrote: "I learn with pleasure that you visit mother frequently, that you keep her company, that you say some prayers together and do some reading and chat together a bit. Thus the time will pass in a gentle and holy manner for the love of God."

On January 3, 1842, sending New Years greetings to his oldest sister, he says:

My New Year's wishes will reach you at Nantes a bit late. But I wish you to know that, in spite of the tardiness of my letters, I thought of you and of the whole family at the beginning of this new year. I begged our Lord that He would bestow His blessings on all the family. The thought occurs to me that I can do so more effectively now that I am approaching nearer the altar. And I assure you that during all these feast days you have been present in my mind. I like to recall the wish that my brother Louis made to my mother when he told her that he wanted all of us to be a family of saints. My dear sister, I think that we cannot better express our good wishes at the beginning of a new year.

He addressed, one after the other, all the members of the family, letting his written words take the place of friendly conversations at the far-off fireside. The merry tone mingled agreeably with edifying traits, especially when he wrote to his nephews and nieces, whose earnest prayers he asked at the approach of his ordination. He received tonsure on March 21, 1842, and minor orders the next December 17.

Francis' kind heart did not forget the family feast days. As the various dates came round, he never failed to send to each one his good wishes and the assurance of a special remembrance at the foot of the altar.

The memory of the faithful servants of the family was also present in his mind. From childhood he was accustomed to consider them part of the household, and nothing that concerned them left him indifferent. A letter from his mother told him of a devoted servant, the good Marion, who had just died. At once he wrote to her sister that he shared her grief and at the same time wished to know whether anything remained due her.

By a letter from my mother I have learned that Marion died about ten days ago after an attack of apoplexy which came on her while she was in Holy Cross Church. I have prayed the good God for her and I have recommended her soul to the prayers of the community. I did not think, when I left Nantes, that poor Marion was so near her end. But I am confident that death found her well prepared. Mother has asked me to let her know whether I had payed her wages when I left Nantes. I did indeed pay her, but a little account remains to be regulated. This I have put off until next year.

This little account refers to a possible arrears of the sum of six francs to be added to the ordinary wages. However small the amount may be, it can be verified. Mother can see in her account book what is due Marion and compare this amount with what you must have found in the little bag that I sent her a year ago. In this bag you should find a little note indicating the amount that it contained. When writing to mother I did not mention this matter. You know that all these little affairs annoy her.

In the St. Sulpice parish the young seminarian was assigned to teaching the catechism of perseverance for girls. To this task he brought the same devotion as to that of the almsgiving which fell to his lot. This latter office was especially pleasing to his charitable soul, and the poor always found a choice place in his heart.

Francis was to be ordained priest on December 27, 1844, and his fervor increased each day. But before the arrival of that joyful day, God had a sad trial for him. In November he received alarming news about his mother's health. As he himself was ill at that very time, he could not go to her bedside. Her condition became rapidly worse. Francis wrote to his brother-in-law as follows:

Today at noon I received your letter informing me of my mother's critical condition. God's holy and loving will be done. I should have wished to go to mother's bedside. But your advice halted me, as I fear I would be too late in setting out. I wait impatiently for your letter tomorrow. If it brings me news of mother's death, I will bless the good God who thus deprives me of the consolation of seeing her once again and especially of seeing her when I am a priest. If she expressed the least desire to see me, I think you would hasten to let me know. I am well enough to undertake the journey. I await your letter tomorrow to make my decision.

The following day (November 9) Francis learned that his excellent mother had left this world without being able to give him a last embrace. His grief was immense, but supported in a Christian manner. He was unable to join his family in paying the last duties to her whom he loved so much, he could not mingle his tears with those of his sister, his brother-in-law, and his nephews, but his thought joined them all in this profound sorrow, and his letters became even more consoling and affectionate than usual.

My dear sister, I have just received the letter from my brother which informs me that God has called our good mother to Himself. May His holy and loving will be done. The letter I received yesterday left me very little hope, and I was prepared for the sacrifice which the good God asks of us. Once again, dear sister, may His holy and loving will be done. He has willed to deprive me of the happiness of seeing my mother one last time. He has denied me the happiness of offering the holy sacrifice in

24

her presence. At least the first Mass that I shall have the happiness to offer will be for her and our father, because I cannot separate the memory of one from that of the other. The good God called father to Himself at almost this same date five years ago.

Five days later he wrote again:

I wrote to you Saturday after learning the news of our good mother's death. Since then I have frequently found myself united with you, with the whole family, asking God that He receive her into His glory, that He receive also our good father, who was taken from us to pass to a better life, five years ago tomorrow. How consoling are the thoughts of our faith in these moments of separation! According to brother Louis' words, which I am fond of recalling, may we strive to form a family of saints.

Among mother's papers you must have found her will. I think she made but few individual bequests. We should consider that our duty is to conform to them fully. Probably she left a letter for me. If so, please send it to me as soon as possible. I long to have these last words of so good a mother.

Francis hastened to carry out her least wishes and even to go beyond them. To his brother-in-law he wrote:

You know that mother was always fond of assisting the poor. And you write me that they were at her funeral in large numbers. I think that the best way to honor her memory, after having the Masses offered that she has asked, would be to distribute some alms according to her intention and that of my father. The following is my thought

25

in the matter: to send to the pastors of la Bruffière, les Landes, Montigné, and Boussay a sum of . . . to each, asking them to distribute this amount according to their good judgment among the poor of their parish, adding thereto an offering for a High Mass which they will be asked to celebrate for my father and my mother. With regard to the pastor of Boussay, since this is the parish where we live and where mother did so much good, I think that we should send him twice the amount that we send to each of the others. In suggesting this alms to you, dear brother, I am thinking of entering into your wishes; yet, as an ecclesiastic and as a deacon specially charged with the care of the poor, according to the primitive institution of my order, I would ask you to leave to my charge the larger part when we regulate our inheritance.

Shortly afterward he thanked his brother-in-law for accepting his suggestion. "I am glad that you have approved the thought which I communicated to you about the distribution of alms in the parishes where we have most of our property."

Only a few days now separated Francis from his ordination to the priesthood. Before starting his retreat, he wrote again to his oldest sister:

This is my last letter to you before I enter upon my retreat in preparation for ordination. I tell myself that the whole family will pray for me during these holy days and will storm heaven to obtain for me the graces which I need on the eve of being elevated to the priesthood. But be assured also that, when I have the privilege of offering the divine sacrifice, I will beseech our Lord to return to you all the good you have done for me by your prayers.

My first remembrance, as likewise yours, will be for my father, my mother, and all those who are dear to us and whom we have lost, or rather who have gone ahead of us to the heavenly fatherland, as I hope by the grace of God.

But, while praying for our dear departed, bear in mind also that I will pray for you all, you to whom the good God has willed to join me in this life, for you my sister, for my brother, for my nephews and nieces.

The Assumption chapel, where Francis had taught catechism to the girls of St. Sulpice parish, preserves the memory of his first Mass (December 28, 1844). The next day Father Richard thanked all those "who had the charity to grant him their prayers, at a time when he was so much in need of them, and who will continue them, since the obligations of the priest increase with the graces he receives from God. I often think I can now show my thanks by praying for them at the holy sacrifice. This will no longer be my poor, wretched prayers that I offer to God for them, but the very prayers of our Lord and of the whole Church which I can dispose of as a priest."

Then the memory of his mother takes his pen. He writes:

I had kept the hope that the good God would leave her in this world long enough that I might have the happi-

27

ness of offering the holy sacrifice in her presence. But He has disposed otherwise, according to His ever loving will. And I believe that she prayed for me during those days when I had special need of prayers. Every day the memory of her is with me at the altar.

The years will pass without weakening in the heart of this loving son the image of his excellent mother. She is the one who, with a gentle and firm hand, trained the great soul of her Francis, as she gave the example of every virtue to her grandchildren.

Even in his last years, Cardinal Richard did not fail to remember the anniversaries of his parents' death, November 8 and 13, and to ask of those about him a memento in their prayers. In the course of his long life, he had a like solicitude for all his departed relatives, and his heart was equally divided between his family on earth and that in the other world.

CHAPTER III

First Years in the Ministry

FATHER RICHARD wished to make a fourth year of theological studies at Paris. His superiors encouraged the idea. But his precarious health, which was hard tried in the last months of 1844, was a serious obstacle to that project. In a letter to his family, he wrote: "I have gone to say Mass at Loretto, to beg the Blessed Virgin that she will decide the matter of my returning to Nantes or my staying in Paris."

His physical condition would be unable to stand the seminary regime. Hence arose a plan to send him to the Marie Therese Infirmary. From there he would come to the seminary every day for his classes.

Regarding this plan, he consulted the Bishop of Nantes, who wanted his prompt return, his brother-in-law, in whom he had great confidence, and his nephew Louis, who was finishing his medical studies in Paris. To his brother-in-law he wrote as follows:

Monday I shall go to live at Marie Therese and shall there await the Bishop's orders. I assure you that I am as ready to leave as to remain, and my only desire is to do the will of God, which will be manifested by that of my superiors. If I considered going to Marie Therese, that was because the fathers at the Seminary urged me to take this step and because Louis, as a doctor, also judged it would be as favorable for my health as the return to Nantes, and perhaps even more so. I ask you to see with Louis what you may judge the more suitable. I should be loath to do anything that might be contrary to God's holy will, but I also do not wish, through my own fault, to miss the chance to complete my studies, a chance which I am not likely to find again.

And a few days later:

I cannot tell you how much I am touched by the interest you show in your last two letters, and your concern for my health. You may be sure that I will entirely conform to the advice you give me with so much wisdom and consideration, and I will take pains to consult Louis as I have already done, when any doubt arises about what my strength will permit me to do. I write you today from the Marie Therese Infirmary, where I came to live yesterday morning. In a few days I shall be better able to give you an account of the sort of life I lead here. The time of rising and going to bed is entirely free. Louis advised me to take eight hours of sleep, and I am following his instruction. Each of us here takes his meals privately in his own room. At eight o'clock I have breakfast with chocolate; at noon dinner; in the evening we have supper at five o'clock. My regime is as good as I could wish for. Louis has already given you a detailed account of the location of the house, and the gardens. We are a twenty-minute walk from St. Sulpice. Our way takes us through the Luxemburg. In bad weather, we can take a bus that passes our door. I have had made for me what they call here "claques," a kind of overshoe to be worn in wet weather. At the Seminary I have kept a room where I can have a fire while waiting for class time and where I can rest a while if I need to. My studying will become less tiring for me since I shall do a considerable amount of it while I am taking walks. Here we go in and out as we wish, quite as we would if we were living in a private house.

I think that at Nantes they may be mistaken about Father de Courson's idea. His intention, as you must suppose, was never that I should remain in Paris at the risk of endangering my health, but, seeing the importance of completing my studies and also seeing, according to Louis' opinion, that my living at Marie Therese removed the obstacles in the matter of my health, he is in accord with this plan. At first he wanted me to go to Nantes and rest there a while, not that my health is as poor as you feared according to his letter to M. Féret, but rather to take your advice and then to return to Paris. I confess that I did not greatly relish that journey to Nantes for a few days only or a few weeks. I would thus lose much time from my studies; the journey at this season would probably tire me; furthermore, once at Nantes I would probably find difficulty in taking much rest, as I would have to engage at least in teaching catechism or something of that sort. Therefore I think that things are arranged for the best through my living at Marie Therese. The fatigue

31

that I experienced at the time of my ordination has left me and now for several days I have felt well. The fever did not return. In short, I feel that my health has improved during the last two months.

With perfect submission Father Richard accepted, a few weeks later, a complete change of program, dictated by his superiors. He obeyed joyously and, when announcing to his family his coming return to Brittany, he did not even hint the least suspicion of regret at abandoning the intellectual advantages offered by residence in Paris.

Probably you already know that the Bishop is calling me back to Nantes and that, instead of remaining at Marie Therese for some time, as I thought I would do, in a few days I shall have the pleasure of seeing you again. I assure you that, notwithstanding the desire and need which I felt to remain still in Paris, this thought of finding myself again in the midst of you so soon is most agreeable to me. I set out for Nantes with pleasure, certain of doing the will of God, which cannot be more clearly manifested to me than by the Bishop's order. Saturday I went to reserve my place in the stagecoach and I shall leave on Monday, February 10, at eight o'clock in the morning. I think we arrive the next day at Nantes at six or seven o'clock in the evening.

Upon his return to Nantes, in the Lent of 1845, he was appointed honorary canon of the cathedral, and was installed in that dignity on March 23,

Easter Sunday. He then entered upon the exercise of the priestly ministry by beginning, in St. Peter's parish, the catechism of perseverance, such as he had done at St. Sulpice. Two of his friends, Father Lemortellec and Father Peigné, helped him in this work, which was quite successful. But the number of souls that it reached was too limited for the zeal of these young apostles. Their looks turned sadly to the young apprentices, numerous at Nantes, who were daily exposed to the dangers of the street, deprived at so early an age of religious instruction and good counsel. The patronages did not yet exist. These priests had the first idea of them and they founded for working boys the society of Our Lady of Joys. Perhaps this title was chosen to recall an ancient shrine in the city of Nantes; perhaps it was prompted by the chapel where the people of Clisson and the neighboring parishes like to pray.

At the Catholic Congress of Lyons in 1874, Father Peigné set forth the beginnings and success of this undertaking. We cannot do better than quote his own words:

In the month of September, 1845, three young priests were called by divine Providence to found the work of Our Lady of Joys. One of them was Father Charles Lemortellec, a priest of remarkably fine mind and heart,

33

whom death took from us at the age of thirty-five. The other was Father Francis Richard de la Vergne, who has become the holy bishop of Belley. The oldest of the three was myself.

At Easter of the preceding year we had given a special retreat to a hundred young apprentices. In the ardor of our young priesthood, we were deeply affected by the unfortunate condition of these poor boys, so exposed to corruption and the loss of faith. At first we thought merely to offer them the modest help of a weekly instruction, known as the catechism of perseverance, fixing the time for eleven o'clock every Sunday morning and feast day, because almost all of them were then victims of that deplorable practice of cleaning up the workshops and putting them in order on Sunday mornings.

One of us used to say Mass for them, another gave them a short instruction, and a third gave them counsel, very much as is done at the catechism classes of St. Sulpice in Paris.

At the end of a few months, we had to recognize that we were producing little fruit because our poor apprentices, in their associations of the afternoon, lost all the good that we strove to produce in them in the morning.

Then He who deigned to become Himself a little apprentice and who told His Apostles, "Let the little children come to me," prompted us to create a new work which until then we had not thought of.

We saw the boys of comfortable families going forth joyously on Sundays, about the middle of the day, to have their games and pastimes in some park near the city or out in the country. We said to one another: Why should we not procure for our boys, disinherited by fortune, the happiness of having their own little country house?

34

FIRST YEARS IN THE MINISTRY

Our deliberation was not long. Only one question remained to be solved: we had no money. A few days later, I had occasion to speak about our great project in a certain wealthy family, that highly approved it. As I mentioned quite simply the little difficulty that held us back, the excellent lady of the house interrupted me and said: "Father, is that all that is holding you back? Right away start a subscription of five francs a year and I will have the honor to write my name at the head of the list." The advice was at once followed. Our good Bishop de Hercé kindly gave his approval and his subscription. He then personally wrote a warm recommendation of the work. Soon three hundred signatures assured us of an annual fund of 1,500 francs, and we lost no time in buying part of a garden. Our new playground measured about 200 feet on a side.

In two or three days we had the place fenced in, and on the following Sunday we invited our happy boys to come and take possession of their new domain. To tell you with what joy they hastened to the meeting place would be useless. After singing a hymn of thanksgiving to the Blessed Virgin and making her the Queen and Mistress of the little place, under the name of Our Lady of Joys, we gave the signal, and a game of prisoner's base began. We began running here and there over the soft ground. At every step our feet uprooted some unfortunate cabbage or some poor carots, quite surprised at this brutal treatment.

At that time we were far from imagining the future which our Blessed Mother had in store for our little work. Father Lemortellec and I patiently dragged our plow and marked out the furrow; Father Richard, who had fallen ill and was suffering severe pain, planted the heavenly seed of his patience and his prayers.

Father Richard's threatened health presently obliged him to take a complete rest in the country. The place of his boyhood held two attractions for him: he liked to live its life, and especially to take part in the religious ceremonies. On April 8, 1845, a special feast day was held at Boussay for the solemn blessing of the church bells. The largest, Marie Appolline, had for its sponsors the Marquise de la Bretesche and M. Louis Pellerin de la Vergne; Canon Richard and his oldest sister were sponsors of the second bell and gave it the name of their little sister, Marie Rosalie.

Bodily sufferings increased for the young priest without exhausting his patience. An accident to his foot obliged him to give up walking for the time. He made a short stay with one of his relatives at the Clairay estate. From there he wrote to one of his nieces who was also suffering: "The good God is giving both of us a grace by sending us a little piece of His cross. Blessed are those who have to suffer something for the love of our Lord. Besides, this good Master knows so well how to soften by the unction of His grace all the pains and sufferings of this life." Shortly afterward an attack of erysipelas confined him to the house at la Vergne and kept him from celebrating Mass.

His physical weakness prevented him from the

36

regular exercise of the ministry. Father de Courson, who had become superior of St. Sulpice, advised him to go to Rome and there continue his studies which he was unable to finish at Paris. The doctors likewise urged him to seek the recovery of his strength in the mild Italian climate. Thus Providence turned his steps toward the Eternal City.

CHAPTER IV

Rome

IN those days a journey from Nantes to Rome was
no small undertaking. There were no express
trains to carry the traveler speedily on his way. But
journey by stagecoach and by boat, in spite of its
inconveniences, had the advantage of giving the
traveler time to admire the beauties of the country
and to become acquainted with points of interest
along his route. Even before leaving France, he
cultivated the practice of making pilgrimages,
which he subsequently continued almost daily in
Italy.

The young priest left Nantes in October, 1846.
A stop at Saumur enabled him to say Mass at Notre
Dame des Ardilliers. At Lyons he visited the shrine
of Fourvière, the prison of St. Pothinus, and the
column of St. Blandina. On November 10 he
reached Marseilles by boat. The next day he sailed
for Leghorn, arriving there on the twelfth. Two
days later he was at Rome.

On November 18, the feast of the Dedication of the Basilica of St. Peter, for the first time he set foot in that impressive church. He experienced a memorable joy at finding himself at the center of the living Church, surrounded by memorials that are dear to all Christians. As formerly at the St. Sulpice Seminary, so now his thought carried him back to Brittany. He was eager to receive news from members of his family and he poured out his heart in long cordial letters, which enabled them in spirit to visit with him the city of the Apostles or to accompany him on his many pilgrimages.

The letters to his nephew Charles, the companion of his early studies and of his whole youth, often reached the proportions of a newspaper. In his first letter he says:

"My dear Charles, it is time to close this letter, which seems to be without end. But I like to have you share my experiences and to begin those chats which we will later have together. . . . I hope to bring back from Rome for you some engravings that will give you a better idea than all my descriptions." But those descriptions were detailed and pleasantly mingled with spiritual reflections.

Father Richard's leisure hours were not many, most of his time being absorbed by his theological studies, to which he devoted himself with his habit-

39

ual sense of duty. His knowledge of Italian was of advantage to him by facilitating his gaining a more thorough knowledge of theology and canon law.

But his physique was not robust enough for him to stand the Roman climate in the summer. During that season of excessive heat, he visited Italy, especially the places of pilgrimage, where he would find the footprints of the saints. His letters take us with him to the different churches of Rome and to the catacombs, then to Monte Cassino with its memories of St. Benedict, to Capua, Naples, Pagani, Salerno, Cava; at Amalfi to the tomb of St. Andrew; among the ruins of Pompeii and Herculaneum; to Tivoli, where he honored the memory of St. Symphorosa and her seven martyr sons; then a visit to Venice and the neighboring islands filled him with the pleasantest memories, as did his visit to Milan. Writing to his nephew Charles, he says:

"The church of St. Mark surpasses everything I have seen. I had the happiness of twice celebrating Mass at the altar of your patron saint, whose relics are in a chapel of the crypt. As you would suppose, the thought of you naturally came to me in the church of St. Charles."

His pilgrimage to Loreto was particularly gratifying to him. He writes:

The church of Loreto is not at all satisfying, perhaps because they have been obliged to reconstruct part of it while keeping some portions of the older structure. But the Holy House, which is enclosed in it, gives it a value not possessed by the most magnificent basilicas. The poor house of Nazareth is always the chief and most precious shrine for the devotion of the pilgrims. I will never stop thanking our Lord for the grace of spending a few weeks near this venerated shrine.

With his usual graciousness and consideration the young priest cheerfully accommodated himself to whatever circumstances he met on his way. He writes:

On all my journeys Providence has always guided me well, and I see that we can never do better than trust fully to that same Providence. Wherever I have passed, I found people ready to do a kind service. At Venice I lodged with an excellent family and, fortunately for my wardrobe, the good lady, Madame Morosini, had a bent for mending. She made a complete inspection of my clothes and put them in perfect condition. In particular she did a magnificent repair job on my overcoat, which has thus recovered an air of youth which it lost during my travels.

For his pilgrimages, especially in the vicinity of Rome, Father Richard at times adopted primitive means of travel. His naturally gay spirit is reflected in his amusing accounts, such as the following:

41

Each of us took an *asinello,* as the Italians call the beast. Three guides accompanied us, shouting at the top of their voice. With us was a Benedictine father, humbly mounted, like us, on an ass. I assure you it was a curious cavalcade, one which now and then caused us distractions during our prayers, which each one said as best he could. . . .

To reach Capua, where the railroad starts, we used a *vetturino.* We saw drive up to our door a vehicle that somewhat resembled a hack, made venerable by long service. We imagined that it could not accommodate more than four persons. In fact, we were only four inside, but two travelers were accommodated in front, and two others behind, not counting two women and a bambino who found a way to travel in a sort of net suspended under the carriage.

Upon leaving Salerno we were installed in a *calessio,* a sort of carriage on two wheels, an ancient vehicle. The livery of our coachman was not such as to offend against ecclesiastical simplicity. He was barefoot and wore a jacket worn with age; it was more holes than jacket.

My route to Rome was by way of Palestrina. If you want to know, my dear Charles, how people travel in the mountains of Italy, here is a little description of my equipage. I was passably well seated on a mule, with a rope serving as reins. Ahead of me walked the guide, in mountaineer's full dress: sugar-loaf hat, short pants, sandals of buffalo skin fastened with cords like buskins. But he was not carrying a gun. You should know that the people of this district like to carry a gun on their shoulder. Thus the two of us traveled for part of the day, now climbing to the very top of the hills, now descending to the depths of the ravines. To right and left we could see villages located in most picturesque positions. My guide was always particular to tell me their names, as also the

42

name of each hill or mountain. And he frequently referred to the illustrious (more or less) personages that he had conducted on his mules.

The memory of these pilgrimages always remained fresh in Father Richard's mind. Half a century later, in the intimacy of family gatherings, the good Cardinal would charm his little grandnephews by his accounts of those experiences. "In those days, my little ones, people traveled gently; they could make friends as they went along. I recall having stayed at a house where the children were numerous, as they are here. When I asked their names, the parents answered: 'This one is Primo, this is Secundo, Tertio, Quarto, Quinto, etc.' Thus each bore his number in proper order."

At Rome what particularly claimed Father Richard's affection was the catacombs. He wrote:

I do not forget my promise to take you to the catacombs. So far we have seen the catacombs of St. Pontian, St. Lawrence, St. Priscilla, St. Peter, St. Marcellinus, St. Agnes. Our regular guide is a Neapolitan peasant, Angelo Capponi, who began working in the catacombs thirty years ago and is now at the head of the workers there. He is a man of good sense and fine spirit, full of faith. He has not fallen into disrespectful familiarity with the saints, even though he touches their bodies, we might say, every day. We like to make him talk. Almost always he has some interesting stories to tell us. One day he was guiding two ladies, recent converts to the faith. All the time they were in the

43

catacombs they kept crying. Upon coming out, they tried to kiss Angelo's hand, which had touched the bodies of so many saints, and they asked him for his blessing. "In their newly found faith," said Angelo as he told us this story, "they had made me a bishop."

With unfailing graciousness Father Richard always tried to satisfy the wishes expressed by the nephews and nieces who had been educated along with him.

"Thank Léonide for the letter she wrote me. Tell her that the copies of the Holy Face which she asked me to get for her are now ready. As to the drawings, I can the better take up the matter since one of the artists who is engaged on these articles of piety is living here with us."

In the Cardinal's room at la Vergne they still keep one of the drawings that he brought back from Rome in June, 1849. It is a guardian angel presenting one of the elect to the Lord and rejoicing over his victory. This little group is taken from Fra Angelico's Last Judgment, a masterpiece on wood, which is in the picture gallery of the Corsini Palace at Rome.

The political events in France had a painful repercussion in northern Italy. Revolution was threatening. In that year 1848, it overthrew the Papal States, piling up murder and ruins. Father

44

Richard's heart grieved at the outrages committed against the Church in the person of its head. But amid those tragic events, after the example of Pius IX, he remained calm and serene.

The close of the year 1848 saw the political situation at Rome still further aggravated. Father Richard writes:

The newspapers have already told you of the death of M. Rossi. This assassination, deliberate and perpetrated so barbarously, stupefied Rome. You can hardly understand how sad this 16th of November has been for all Catholic hearts. For many centuries no one had seen such an outrage against the Holy See—a fire started against one of the gates of the palace, a canon set up in the square to threaten the Supreme Pontiff: such are some of the circumstances of that sad day, which will ever be to the shame of those who behaved with such excess against a Pope who has never done anything but good to them. Pray for the Church and for the Holy Father, who, we are told, amid all these tumults preserves a spirit of resignation that shows the holiness of his soul. The good God seems to have chosen him as an innocent victim to expiate the sins of his people. The future is more uncertain than ever; but God is watching over His Church. St. Peter will not desert Rome. The city of the Apostles and martyrs will, I hope, again see days of joy and triumph.

In spite of the political events, Father Richard planned to prolong his stay in Rome, when he was recalled by Father Féret, the director of the Nantes seminary, and by his family, who were disturbed

45

on account of the Italian Revolution. On March 25 he started back for France, sailing from Civitavecchia. His physical condition, though improved, still required caution. To avoid the sudden change of climate from sunny Italy to foggy Brittany, he decided to make his return journey in gentle stages.

Again he stopped at certain beloved shrines: Notre Dame de la Garde, Avignon, Fourvière. Then the vicinity of Annecy drew him to the tomb of his patron saint in spite of the snow that still covered Savoy.

Before returning to Nantes, Father Richard wished to visit his spiritual director, Father de Courson, at Paris. Then, after a retreat and a brief journey in Belgium, he came back to his native city, where his family and his ecclesiastical superiors were awaiting him.

CHAPTER V

Vicar General of Nantes

(1850–1870)

BISHOP DE HERCÉ had planned to attach Father Richard to his own person. But the venerated prelate died on January 31, 1849, a few months before the young priest's return to France. Bishop Jaquemet, the new bishop of Nantes, had known Father Richard at St. Sulpice and had not forgotten him. Presently he appointed him to the office of vicar general, left vacant by the premature death of Father Vrignaud. Father Richard was only thirty-one years old. In his humility, he was astonished to find himself so soon charged with that important office. But at the bishop's house he would find the life of labor and recollection which so well suited his personal tastes.

Bishop Jaquemet was a gentle soul. Separated from his earthly family, for whom he had a deep affection, he wished to form a spiritual family by

47

gathering his vicars and his secretaries about him, in an intimate community. The episcopal family included seven priests. Notwithstanding differences of character, perfect harmony prevailed among these chosen priests who, later on separated by circumstances, preserved the memory of those years spent together in common under the fatherly authority of their bishop. Bishop Jaquemet himself speaks of it in a letter to his family, saying: "You can easily form an idea of the bishop's house at Nantes. We are eight, but we have only one heart and one soul. During part of every meal we have some interesting reading. The days are filled with work, but my beloved sons are so fond of one another that weariness is forgotten as soon as they assemble together with me."

Of the old bishop's palace nothing remains except the square tower, close to the cathedral. On the second floor of it Father Richard occupied a modest room, which was without any superfluous comforts. Nothing less than the Bishop's command made him keep a fire there during the harsh winter months.

The young priest's days were filled with intense labor, beginning at dawn. He rose at four o'clock to make his meditation, after which he went to the cathedral. The people attending the five o'clock

Mass used to see his tall silhouette on the walls of
the church while he was devoutly making his stations of the cross.

Upon returning to his room, he at once became
absorbed in his duties and put his whole soul and
conscience into the many details of his office, without ever thinking of any rest. The Bishop, seeing
Father Richard's excessive labor and concerned
for his health, decided that every day, after the
morning meal, the episcopal family should take a
short recreation in the little garden. To these gatherings Father Richard brought his gentle courtesy
and his habit of preferring to be always in the back-
ground. Usually he had with him a quantity of
documents about which he asked the advice of the
other priests. Thus even his moments of relaxation
were a continuation of study and labor. Bishop
Jaquemet despaired at not being able to teach his
vicar to take some rest. But, as he used to say, "he is
the half of my soul." The prelate rightly appreci-
ated his devoted vicar and in full confidence entrusted him with a large part of the administration
of the diocese.

Father Richard quickly acquired an immense influence over the clergy. The older priests received
from him a welcome full of deference; and the
youngest were put at ease by his cordial benevo-

lence. He knew how to give advice and encouragement, and he impressed all by his humility, his uprightness, and his supernatural spirit. During a retreat of the pastors, upon leaving a conference at which Father Richard had given certain admonitions in the name of Bishop Jaquemet, a good pastor exclaimed: "Our beloved vicar general is only a simple priest like us; but he has such a sway over us and is so revered by us that, if he should ask us to walk across burning coals, we would want to obey him."

In his own home Father Richard had learned that exquisite gentleness is consonant with firmness in the guidance of those one loves. And he acted thus in his whole administration. He wanted perfect discipline and knew how to obtain it. No one disregarded his orders, and he was even considered severe. But whenever he had to act with rigor, he did not yield to any human prompting, but obeyed solely his conscience. Evidently he was concerned simply with fulfilling his duty, for the greater good of those whom he had to reprehend. His authority brought obedience because it was based on complete forgetfulness of self and of his personal interests.

When receiving priests of the diocese, the young vicar general never forgot that he was merely the spokesman of his Bishop. More than once he was obliged to detect the ill-disguised deception on the part of some priest who came to see the Bishop. But because of the Bishop's unsettled health, the priest would find that he could interview only the vicar general. With the utmost affability, Father Richard would endeavor to appease the visitor's disappointment.

If he had to communicate to some priest a favorable reply of the Bishop, he always attributed to the Bishop the agreeable part of the decision: "The Bishop is pleased to grant your request." But when a refusal had to be given, he took the blame on himself: "I regret that I cannot grant your request."

Father Richard was not surprised that a priest should need light and guidance in the difficulties of the ministry. Most graciously he offered each one the help of his experience. The simplicity of his welcome quickly put at ease those who had to consult him often, and they had no difficulty in laying their whole mind open to him. One day a seminarian, a protégé of his, being in his room and seeing on the shelves of his library a fine edition of Carrières and Menochius, remarked: "If I only had a copy of that work, how it would help me in my Scripture study!" "Do you indeed think it would be of great help to you? Very well," said the vicar general kindly, "take it with you." And he handed the volume to the young man.

The Bishop also assigned to Father Richard the charge of the schools of the diocese. Eleven of these existed at that time: the preparatory seminary; St. Stanislas, La Salette, Notre Dame des Couëts, the preparatory seminary of Guérande, the junior colleges of Chateaubriant, Machecoul, la Ducherais, and Chauvé. The college of Ancenis was reopened and, at the same period, the day-school for Nantes children was founded.

The vicar general bestowed the most devoted care on these establishments. Every month he visited the colleges at Nantes and, at least twice a year, in March and at the close of the school year, he made his regular visits to the schools that were at a distance. Taking the professors one by one, he asked each, with fatherly kindness, what were his difficulties, what were his wishes. To some he gave needed counsel, to others a word of encouragement, reminding all that they were working for God, and that their Bishop loved them, blessed them, and thanked them for their devoted labors.

To the pupils also he showed the kindest interest. His reliable memory enabled him to recall the grades of many students, a trait which helped him to follow their individual progress. If the school was having recreation when he arrived, they at once gathered round him. He would say to them: "My dear children, I cannot embrace you all, as I would wish, but I will embrace the first in each class in the name of all the rest." In 1861 he did this at the St. Joseph Institution at Ancenis. Seeing a tall boy for the seventh grade coming to him, he received him kindly, but also expressed his surprise, saying: "Where is that good little fellow John Baptist Jamin, who last year was at the head of the sixth grade? Has he fallen back to second place this year?" He was then told that Jamin was still first but was then sick, and that the second came in his place.

We have the following testimony of an eyewitness:

When he used to visit us, what we pupils considered most dominant in him was his fatherly kindness, his evident fondness for us. We could see that, in coming to us, his only desire was to do us good. His holiness depicted on his face struck us and raised us toward heaven. And so we held him in veneration.

One day, in the spring of 1860 or 1861, after returning from Rome, he was relating to us the impressions he had during an audience with the Holy Father. He said: "You could see shining on the forehead of Pius IX a glow of holiness, something of a divine sort that called for respect but that, instead of preventing your being at ease, gave you a feeling of gentle and filial confidence." When we left the chapel, several of the boys said to one another:

53

"What he said about Pius IX is precisely what we note in himself; and he produced the very same effect on us while he was talking to us."

When addressing the boys of the different schools, Father Richard had a particular charm that won their attention. On examination days the most timid were put at ease by his fatherly kindness. He had an exquisite way of insinuating a lesson, of inserting an edifying word or a practical counsel in the midst of a conversation.

In 1865, in the name of Bishop Jaquemet, he presided at the distribution of awards at the Day School for Children of Nantes. A regrettable accident prevented those present from hearing the young orator who was to deliver the usual discourse. Father Richard was able to turn the incident to good account by simply taking the orator's place. The boy was to show the genius of Racine and the influence of religion upon the seventeenth century. The year before, on a like occasion, the speaker had set forth the influence of that same religion upon the mind of the great Basil. Between that light of the Greek Church and that glory of Christian France, Father Richard placed the memory of St. Augustine, the first of the Latin fathers, the former professor of Milan and Rome. Augustine, raised to the see of Hippo, writing to one of his former pupils, spoke about their studies of earlier days and, said Father Richard, as he turned toward the youngest of the boys, "even about passive infinitives and supines in -um, as well as about great philosophical truths. Only the truth can teach what is true. But the truth is Christ. Give yourselves, then, to Christ, our Lord and Master."

A few days later he was presiding at a similar ceremony at the preparatory seminary. This time the orators depicted in outline the pontificates of Pius V, Pius VI, Pius VII, and Pius IX. Father Richard expressed his congratulations to the young orators for the eloquent and earnest way they had treated their magnificent subjects. In the course of his address he introduced a few recollections that he brought back from Rome. He said:

Not long ago I chanced to see an old document of Peter II, Duke of Brittany, in which the new Duke, after the example of his predecessors, sent to the Supreme Pontiff the homage of his loyal obedience. In a Latin which has not perhaps all the purity and elegance of Ciceronian style, Peter II expressed to the Holy Father his feelings and those of his people, saying that the "Bretons *servaverunt se et perseveraverunt sine variatione in obedientiis suis erga Sanctam Sedem* ("The Bretons have preserved and persevered without alteration in their obedience toward the Holy See"). And we also, with our faithful subjects, wish ever to be *valde catholici* ("very good Catholics")." We will not go back on those noble protestations of our ancestors, but will retain inviolable that attachment, so strongly rooted in the soil of Brittany, to the Catholic, Apostolic, and Roman Church.

Father Richard spoke from his heart. He had the talent of touching his hearers and making their souls vibrate in unison with his, when he expressed the earnest wish that the faith of the early days should remain living and strong in his beloved Brittany.

Each year, toward the end of the vacation period, the superiors and professors of the educational institutions came together at the major seminary for a special retreat. The vicar general was present, giving an example of regularity and prayer. He then considered the means to increase a fondness for work and for piety.

At the time of its foundation, the Day School for Children of Nantes was established on rue Lafayette in a house which soon proved to be too small for the numerous pupils. The Bishop looked about for more spacious quarters. A proposal was made to transfer this school to a large building that was surrounded with gardens, which the diocesan missioners of St. Francis possessed, and to build a new house for them near the chapel of the Immaculate Conception, which would become theirs. But to carry out this project, the property adjoining

56

the chapel would have to be acquired, and money would have to be found for the building expenses. Immediately Father Richard offered the Bishop the sum of 100,000 francs taken from his personal income, for the foundation of the Missioners of the Immaculate Conception. Many years later, at the time of the separation of Church and state, when the government intended to seize this house, Father Richard, who had become cardinal and archbishop of Paris, reclaimed and recovered his property so as to let the missioners continue to enjoy its use.

The primary schools, too, could count on the vicar general's interest. He was director of an association whose purpose was to procure a Christian education for the children of the working classes. His zeal also helped to increase at Nantes the houses of the Brothers of St. John Baptist de la Salle.

Father Richard was ecclesiastical superior of the religious communities of the diocese. He was consoled and encouraged by the fervor of these holy houses. In 1865 he wrote to the superior of the Carmelite convent: "Together with your sisters, ask our Lord to bless the ministry that He sends me to fulfill in your regard. Only one thing do I request of Him, that I may be a docile instrument in His hands and that my sins may not be an obstacle to the graces which He has prepared for your souls."

The sisters speak of his particular interest in their spiritual direction. They say:

> When we had the grace of having him for our superior and when we consulted him in the parlor about how we should act in such or such circumstances, we used to see this man of God put his hand before his eyes, as though to recollect himself. We could easily see that, before answering us, he was asking Him from whom all light comes.
>
> When Father Richard had to discuss or decide any matter, he always asked us to grant him some time for reflection and for consulting God, that he might know the divine will.

When he noticed too great eagerness in those who sought his advice, he used to say: "Not so fast, not so fast; be calm, so as to act in the spirit of the good God. Let us not stride over Providence, as the good St. Vincent de Paul says."

In 1856 the Congregation of Helpers of the Holy Souls was founded in Paris. The members take a special obligation to pray, suffer, and labor for the souls in purgatory. Bishop Jaquemet asked his vicar general to go to Paris and treat with the foundress, Mother Mary of Providence, for the installation of a house of the community at Nantes. Soon afterward the diocese was enriched by the addition of a new religious family.

Father Richard was also received as a father by the Daughters of Wisdom, the Ursulines, and the Madames of the Sacred Heart. The girls at the boarding school of the last named used to wait impatiently for the visits of the good canon who each time asked for them permission to talk in the refectory for nine days. This practice became habitual and came to be called in the house "Father Richard's novena."

Thus all the communities had their share of the vicar general's zeal; to each he gave generously of his counsel and example, which were always marked by kindness and a supernatural spirit.

According to the desire of Pius IX, the diocese of Nantes was to adopt the Roman liturgy in public worship. In 1852 Father Richard was appointed president of a commission charged with studying this important question, as also with examining the origins of the Church of Nantes and the history of its saints with a view to preparing the Proper of the diocese. For more than four years the vicar general found, in the work of this commission, an added burden to the intense labors which he daily assumed. His tireless energy enabled him to bring this new task to a successful issue.

The Proper of Nantes, once it was drawn up, had to be approved by Rome. Father Richard retained happy memories of Rome from his first years in the priesthood. Hence he experienced a profound joy in accompanying Bishop Jaquemet on his visit *ad limina* in 1857. A few priests and two young men of Nantes, the Marquis de Ternay and M. Charles Pellerin de la Vergne, Father Richard's nephew, accompanied their bishop on this journey, which the vicar general made under different conditions from those of his journey ten years before. The railroad now took the place of the stagecoach. The journey, however, was made gradually. Orleans and Paris were the first stops. The pilgrims climbed the Fourvières hill at Lyons; at Marseilles they visited Notre Dame de la Garde, then the ancient abbey of Saint Victor and the crypt of St. Lazarus.

On April 27 they sailed from Marseilles. As the ship was leaving the harbor, the group from Nantes intoned the *Ave Maris Stella* as a parting salutation to Notre Dame de la Garde. The next day they were at Genoa. They directed their steps to the tomb of St. Catherine and the humble cell where she chose to live in the midst of her beloved poor. They then admired the churches and the marble palaces, especially the Brignolles-Sales Palace, where the mistress of the house, a relative of St. Francis de Sales, gave them a cordial welcome. On the evening of the 28th they set sail again, this time for Leghorn. This stop gave them opportunity to visit Pisa, where they saw the Duomo, the Baptistery, the Campanile, and the Campo Santo. Finally, after one night on the water, the party reached the Papal States at Civitavecchia. Two carriages brought them to the Eternal City by the Via Aurelia. Of a sudden, as they reached the top of a hill, the vetturino announced: "Behold, St. Peter's!" In a spontaneous burst of faith, the travelers stepped out of the carriages, knelt on the ground, and together recited the Credo, the Pater, a prayer to the Blessed Virgin, and an invocation to the great Apostle whose basilica could be seen afar.

Two days later Pius IX received the members of the little group from Nantes with particular benevolence and presented each with a beautiful engraving of one of Michelangelo's Madonnas.

While the pilgrims were enjoying Rome, Father Richard took up his incessant labor to advance the examination and approval of the offices proper to the diocese of Nantes, which he himself had drawn up. Bishop Jaquemet wrote:

Monsignor Capalti, secretary of the Congregation of Rites, is charmed with Father Richard's work. He regards it as a model, superior to anything he has received from France. I think he is going to propose it as a pattern to the other dioceses. What especially struck him was the judicious fidelity to the liturgical traditions. Monsignor Capalti has conceived such an esteem for Father Richard that he wishes to confer with him about other difficult points with which he is concerned.

The month of May passed rapidly amid numerous negotiations. Father Richard himself wrote: "At Rome as at Nantes the days are too short." He could hardly find a few free intervals for visits, with his nephew, to some of his beloved shrines. At length, on June 10, before leaving for France, he witnessed the Corpus Christi procession at Rome.

In 1860 the Roman revolution took another advance in snatching from the Church the last shreds of her States. Pius IX was confronted with the bad faith or the hostility of the political powers; but at sound of his voice volunteers from all countries hastened to defend the Holy See. France sent her best sons, and the diocese of Nantes had the honor of furnishing, along with an important contingent of valiant men, the general who headed the papal army, M. de la Moricière. Father Richard, having seen at Rome the first attacks made on the papacy, resolved to maintain the most loyal devotion to the person of Pius IX. He knew most of the Breton zouaves or at least was acquainted with their families. General de la Moricière had been a charming member of those cordial gatherings at the bishop's house in Nantes and had become a friend of the vicar general. These were sufficient reasons for Father Richard to unite himself in prayer and thought with the heroic struggles of the papal soldiers against the Piedmont forces and the legions of Garibaldi. The fighting at Castelfidardo and the siege of Ancona found a sad echo in his heart. Later when the diocese of Nantes united in offering to General de la Moricière a medal commemorative of his devotedness to the Holy See, Father Richard was chosen to present it to him. Four years after this, Father Richard, in the name of his Bishop, accompanied this valiant Christian to his last resting place and there, beside his grave, expressed the feelings of the clergy.

CHAPTER VI

The Vicar General's Charity

THE duties of the vicar general brought him into relations with all classes of society. At a later date he referred "to those Christians of a noble and ancient race, who were united to me by the most friendly relations of piety and charity." Toward those who aided him in his numerous activities, he was never wanting in any duty of politeness, propriety, zeal, or gratitude. But his goodness inclined him toward those who had need of help. He seemed to take particular pleasure with children, the lowly, the afflicted. In his childhood his father and mother had taken him with them on their visits to the poor and had taught him to aid them with kindness. He was ever ready to hear them, to help them, and to console them.

He used to visit the attics and the most wretched sections of the city, and there distributed his alms with the word of God. One day he found a family that had been brought to Nantes by a succession of misfortunes. In that home the most abject wretchedness was evident. Already two children were dying from lack of fresh air and from other privations. Father Richard became a providence to this poor family. He supplied work and assistance and assumed responsibility for a boy who wished to enter the seminary. At Nantes he provided food for thirty families and visited them as often as possible. The budget of his charities was so large that he reduced his personal expenses to what was strictly necessary. His breviary was plainly bound. Even in the city he wore shoes such as were usually to be seen only on the feet of peasants. In fact he had bought them from a cobbler.

When he went to Boussay, the parishioners saw that his hat was old and much worn. They said: "If we dared, we would buy a new hat for Father Francis; he gives everything away." One winter evening on the streets of Nantes someone saw him take off his own cape and put it on the shoulders of a poor woman who was shivering with the cold. Bishop Jaquemet, noticing that he thus distributed all his income to works of piety and to the poor, forbade him to give away more than a thousand francs without his permission. At times Father Richard would plead the cause of such or such an unfortunate family, one deserving of a rather generous relief. The Bishop interrupted him, saying: "I will permit you to give this help when you have bought some new shirts for yourself."

After his mother's death he sent to a college at Nantes all the silver plate that was his share of the inheritance. To strip himself, to deprive himself of everything, in favor of the unfortunate, became a habit with him. When he was a very young priest, upon his return from Italy, at Nantes a house had been founded for the shelter of girls. Father Richard took special interest in this work and contributed to it as much as he could. One day two ladies came to him to beg in behalf of a lottery organized for this work. The vicar general's purse had responded to so many appeals that at the moment it was quite empty. He sadly watched these ladies go away empty-handed. Then of a sudden he called them back and said to them: "I have something to offer you for your work." Just the day before he had received from Rome a superb chalice which he had ordered made according to his own tastes and ideas. He valued this precious object, but spontaneously gave it for the lottery; it soon became the possession of a curate in Nantes.

Father Richard had accepted an invitation to preach the sermon at the clothing of a Carmelite nun at Nantes. The family of this young lady, in gratitude, presented him with a set of books of considerable value. As soon as these volumes reached him, he wrote the following lines to the young Carmelite novice:

My dear daughter, I write to thank you for the beautiful volumes that you have sent me. Catalini's commentary on the Pontifical is certainly one of the works that could be most acceptable to me and the most useful. Allow me, dear sister, to make it even more useful by not keeping it for my personal use but by putting it in our little library at the bishop's house. I have preached to you the love of poverty. Let me love it a little more for myself. Your beautiful volumes will thus have a double value in my eyes, and I will feel the more obliged to pray for you.

The next year he would not accept the invitation to preach at this same novice's profession except on condition that he should receive nothing by way of gratitude. He wrote to her, saying: "You have freely chosen holy poverty. Allow me to share a little your renunciation of the things of this world."

Father Richard practiced this religious virtue to a high degree. One day when he called on his sister, wearing such a worn cassock that she remarked it, he answered that, for visits to his family, he always put on his best clothes. "This cassock," he said, "is

my best; and just now I cannot buy another."
"Very well," said Madame Pellerin de la Vergne,
"I am going to have one made for you, and you will
be able to be well dressed at least for your visits."
A few weeks later, Father Richard again appeared
dressed in his old cassock. "Francis, what have you
done with your new cassock?" He tried to pass the
matter off as mere thoughtlessness on his part. But
upon his sister's insistence, he had to confess what
had happened. When a certain poor seminarian
called upon him, Father Richard saw that the
young man's cassock was in a sad state indeed. At
once he gave him his own new one, saying: "I
think we are about the same size; here is the very
thing you need."

Father Richard gave not merely all he had, he
gave himself also. He felt a need of spending himself to be useful, to give pleasure to others, to do
good.

In spite of his many occupations, he was able to
take some part in the life of his family. He had
baptized the children of his nephews and nieces.
He took an interest in their studies and gave them
presents of various books adapted to their different ages, always inscribing a little dedication on
the first page. The son of his nephew Charles, the
Benjamin of that new generation, thus received

from him *Les Evangiles et les Actes des Apôtres,* explained by Countess de Ségur to her grandchildren, then a fine copy of the *Vie des saints,* out of which little Albert's pious mother used to read to her son each evening the story of the saint of the day, which was also illustrated with pictures in the book.

Although devoted to all his duties, the vicar general dreaded that he might not have performed them fully. Bishop Jaquemet had noticed this disposition, and wrote: "Father Richard suffers, worn out by excess of work, tormented by the fear that he has not done all he ought to have done. I should like to solace his sadness by showing him that everything is going fine."

Thinking that Father Richard could recuperate his strength in the atmosphere of his home better than anywhere else, Bishop Jaquemet sent him every year, in the month of September, to spend a fortnight at la Vergne. The word of his coming caused great joy in the whole neighborhood. His servants made sure ahead of time to have ready the tenderest pigeons and the freshest vegetables to be served at his table. He gave them a free hand in details of this sort, and without any reflection he used to take whatever was placed before him.

One day he was having dinner at the seminary.

When he had finished eating some boiled eggs, the superior, Father Branchereau, took Father Richard's plate and was about to pass it to the waiter when he noticed that one of the eggs was quite spoiled. Father Richard had eaten it without saying anything. Father Branchereau, admiring this spirit of mortification, appeared not to notice it lest he wound his guest's well-known humility, but afterward at the recreation he related the incident for the edification of the seminarians.

During these vacations at home, Father Richard wished to be regarded at Boussay simply as the other priests, ready to sing the High Mass or preach on Sundays. He said to Father Mérel, the pastor: "I am on vacation, I am here one of your priests, a son of the parish." He retained his exquisite amiability and simplicity.

He came to Boussay, he said, "to sleep and to pray." The second part of this program was always carried out. Every day his celebration of Mass and his recitation of his breviary in the church was an edification to the people of Boussay. In the evening he was careful not to neglect his visit to the Blessed Sacrament. But the time given to sleep was not greatly prolonged. As soon as he reached la Vergne, even before he arrived there, he found the poor, and they were numerous. The holy priest received each of them individually and took note of their needs. Then his farm tenants came to treat directly with him, and many priests came to ask his advice. And he used to visit the cemetery daily, there to pray at the graves of his parents and those of the deceased priests.

One day a priest had come from a distance of about twenty miles to consult the vicar general. But he did not find him at la Vergne or at the rectory or at his steward's. "Wait a moment," said the housekeeper at the rectory, "I will go find him for you." She did, in fact, find him at the bedside of a poor paralytic, kneeling beside the invalid, whom he helped with his words and his alms.

Each day about noon the postman brought the correspondence from the diocesan office. Father Richard examined it and wrote his replies in the evening so that all might be in order the next day. If we add his attention to several matters he had kept for examination at greater leisure during his vacation, we can easily understand that the time he had for rest was very limited.

The farmers of la Vergne were fond of receiving the visits of "Monsieur Francis," and these visits always bore good fruit. At the time of the Crimean War, he asked the pastor of Boussay to accompany him to the home of one of his farmers who was dangerously ill. When the poor dying man saw his master, he made an effort to sit up in bed. "Oh, Monsieur Francis, how glad I am to see you. Monsieur Francis, I have great need of my John to take care of the farm. He is a soldier at Lyons. If you could have him come." "I will see what can be done," replied the priest. "Be comforted and pray to the good God. You see, the good Master will arrange everything, if it ought to be arranged." A few weeks later, John Desfontaines arrived at Ecorchevrières to receive the last words of his dying father.

Apart from vacation, Father Richard occasionally made short visits to his birthplace. Sometimes a few friends accompanied him. One day the people of Boussay were amused at seeing him bring with him a Chinese prince in colorful costume and queue. But his visits were always synonymous with charity. Despite his absorbing priestly occupations, the vicar general endeavored to continue the benevolent works of "Monsieur Francis."

CHAPTER VII

The Last Days of
Bishop Jaquemet

DURING the last ten years of his episcopate,
Bishop Jaquemet suffered continually failing
health. The pastoral burden fell almost entirely on
the shoulders of Father Richard. The glory of God
and the consolation of the prelate, whom he venerated as a father, occupied him ceaselessly. The
august invalid retired to his country house at Talence, and Father Richard resided near him. Early
every morning he could be seen making his way to
the cathedral.

At Nantes they used to say: "We have two bishops, one in purple, the other in black," thus indicating the large part which the vicar general took in
the conduct of the diocese. But everyone admired
the humility of this priest who replied to the confidence and affection of his bishop by the most

filial deference and the most perfect submission and a scrupulous conformity to his orders, as to his least wishes. The two of them had but one heart and one soul. When Bishop Jaquemet was obliged to spend some time at Eaux-Bonnes and at Agen, he carried on a most cordial correspondence with Father Richard, then called him to his side before sending him to make the visit to Rome which he himself was unable to undertake. Many matters had to be treated of with the Holy See. The most important concerned the beatification of the venerable Duchess of Brittany, whose cult had not yet been recognized by a papal decree. A historical and liturgical petition regarding this immemorial cult was drawn up by Father Richard to be submitted to the Holy Father. The bishops of Brittany and of Poitiers, as also the archbishop of Tours, added their petitions to the petition of the diocese of Nantes to obtain the beatification of the servant of God. Father Richard was charged with placing in the hands of the Supreme Pontiff all the necessary documents and the various petitions.

The Bishop of Nantes wrote as follows: "Most Holy Father, owing to the impossibility of myself accomplishing this pious pilgrimage in person, I am deputing in my stead, for the accomplishment of my various duties, the priest who possesses my confidence in the highest degree, my first vicar general, Father Francis Richard. As he has been associated with my labors from the outset of my episcopate, he will be able to answer, as well as I could, all the questions which Your Holiness or the Roman Congregations by your order may wish to ask."

At Rome, where he remained about two months, Father Richard carried out the commissions entrusted to him with his usual fidelity. At an audience, Pius IX, speaking of the beatification of Frances d'Amboise, said to him graciously: "This will be God's recompense to the Bretons for their devotedness to the Catholic Church." The cause was submitted without delay to the Congregation of Rites. Father Richard furnished all the needed explanations. The most complete success crowned his efforts and rewarded his devotion to the holy Duchess.

Another joy was granted him. In the Eternal City a young zouave from Nantes, Joseph Guérin, who had been mortally wounded at Castelfidardo, was the object of a popular cult. In the diocese of Nantes several extraordinary cures were attributed to him. At Rome a cure through his intercession had just taken place, which seemed to all a conspicuous prodigy. Father Richard writes as fol-

75

lows to Bishop Jaquemet: "I am sending you all the details about the miracle that took place in Rome last week through the intercession of the young Guérin. I think we must not long delay taking an active hand in this cause, which is being zealously considered at the Congregation of Rites."

But Providence reserved a trial for the vicar general. Father Féret, superior of the seminary of Nantes, to whom Father Richard was much attached, was suddenly carried off by pneumonia. Bishop Jaquemet wrote: "I am pained at the thought of the blow to Father Richard when he learns the sad news. Happily he is so united to God that he will submit with peaceful resignation."

Then, feeling that the absence of his other self was painful to the members of the episcopal household, the invalid Bishop wrote to them as follows: "Father Richard has left you. This is an additional reason for me to pray that the help of the Holy Spirit may direct all your thoughts and acts. So far as possible, follow the path traced by Father Richard for the time of my absence." A few months later, after his return to Talence, he said: "If I did not have such vicars general and such secretaries, I would at once sign my resignation." His exhaustion thereafter condemned him to the life of a recluse, and kept him from participating in any

76

public functions. Generally Father Richard took his place. At this period we find the name of the vicar general associated with all the religious events of the diocese. He is the one who, at Holy Cross Church, solemnly promulgated the affiliation of Notre Dame of Bon-Secours to Notre Dame of Loretto; he is the one who founded and directed the Association of Christian Fathers. He blessed the school of the Brothers of St. Similianus, the prison chapel, the chapel of the Sisters of Hope, that of the Sisters of Chavagnes at Ancenis, and many others. He presided at the inauguration of the great organ in the chapel of the Immaculate Conception. On every occasion he addressed the faithful, reanimating their zeal for the poor of Nantes, to whom he contributed his help whole-heartedly.

His solicitude extended to all the country parishes and, as often as his busy life permitted, brought him back to the parish of his own boyhood. Father Pineau, of the Immaculate Conception, gave a mission at Boussay in 1862. Father Richard was happy to be present at some of the ceremonies. The next year he presided at the blessing of a beautiful calvary erected near la Vergne in memory of that mission. Toward its cost he contributed generously.

Bishop Mermillod and Bishop de la Hailandière took the place of the sick bishop in administering the sacrament of confirmation. In May, 1864, Father Richard accompanied Bishop de la Hailandière to Boussay, where 366 children were confirmed. The day before the ceremony a large concourse of people greeted the prelate on his arrival and escorted him to the church. He whom they still called "Monsieur Francis" ascended the pulpit to thank the people for the magnificent welcome of our Lord's representative. Then he recalled the cherished bonds that united him to this parish, and the precious memory of the priestly virtues which his boyhood had witnessed there. In the evening the pastor noted in the parish register that "Canon Richard has naturally forgotten only one thing, his own virtues, which not only Boussay but the whole diocese of Nantes witnesses every day in him."

Father Richard's hours were filled with intense labor. Yet he reserved some intervals for a new task. He felt drawn to sketch the life of the Blessed Frances d'Amboise. In the preface of his book he wrote as follows: "Her cult was for me a cult of filial piety, her memory the memory of a mother. Hence I thought not only that I could, but that I should, add my humble stone to the monument which our

78

age is erecting to the glory of the holy Duchess."
Already the cause of beatification had led him to
undertake researches in the libraries and archives
of Brittany. He followed the blessed Duchess step
by step with growing admiration.

It was a conscientious biography, as well as a
work of love. In the Preface the author says:

> We have completed the life of the Blessed Frances. It
> was a labor of love. How good it is to live with the mem-
> ory of the saints! Even after centuries have passed, their
> memory has a fragrance that does not weaken. The more
> we studied this pure and beautiful life, the more we un-
> derstood that only holiness counts for anything. Human
> glory may shine with a brilliant flash, but this flare soon
> grows pale and dies out. The glory of the saints shines
> eternally.

Father Richard gives us, in two volumes of un-
doubted value, the fruit of his long research. But
all this did not satisfy his piety. He strove to make
the life of the holy Duchess known in popular circles by writing an abridged account of her life under the title of *Légende de la Bienheureuse Fran-
çoise d'Amboise*. He said:

> The people of Brittany unanimously bestowed the
> name of "mother" upon the Blessed Françoise d'Amboise,
> and this title comes down to us through the centuries.
> Even in our own days the old men of the village of
> Couëts, near Nantes, who in their boyhood had prayed

79

at the tomb of the saint, called her "the good mother Duchess." We desire to make the account of her life accessible to all so that the Breton people may be able to learn and love in the Blessed Frances the sovereign so beloved by our fathers.

Besides, Frances who during her life bestowed so many favors on our province, who prayed with such persevering fervor for "this poor people of Brittany," as she said with motherly tenderness, has now in God's presence the mission of watching over us and preserving for us the holy traditions of the faith and Christian piety ever living among us. The memory of her holiness is a domestic memory for all our families. Her life teaches them in a charming manner the practice of the virtues. We will find the best guaranty of happiness in this world and in the next in her maxim: Do all things that God may be better loved.

Father Richard's persevering efforts prepared the way for the glorification of the blessed Frances. His soul must have been deeply moved that, at the word of Pius IX, all Brittany acclaimed its sovereign. During the closing days of April and on the first of May, 1866, throngs of people flocked to Nantes, and the festivities of the triduum celebrated in honor of the holy Duchess were magnificent. Several bishops, famous orators, such as Father Hyacinth, Bishop Mermillod, and Father Souaillard, enhanced the brilliance of the ceremonies. In the old cathedral the image of the Carmelite princess stood out above the high altar amid

flowers and lights. Her precious remains, saved
from the fury of the Revolution, were exposed for
the veneration of the faithful in two reliquaries
of rare beauty. At last the great bell of St. Peter's
was heard and, amid an immense and brilliant procession, the statue of the Blessed Frances, raised on
a rich platform, was carried to the ducal château,
then through the streets of Nantes. Frances seemed
once more to be visiting "her good city of Nantes"
to receive the loving homage of her subjects.

On that memorable feast day, in the courtyard
of the château, was sung a cantata which has remained celebrated. The story of it is interesting. A
few days before the triduum, the Vendean poet,
Emile Grimaud, brought to Canon Richard a cantata written at his request in honor of Blessed
Frances. The vicar general said to the author:
"This needs an orchestration. I have heard much
talk of a certain M. Bourgault-Ducoudray, who
lives in rue du Boccage. Go see him." The young
composer received M. Grimaud rather ill and sent
him off with a sharp refusal, declaring that people
do not come three days before the performance to
ask for such a thing to be done. As M. Grimaud was
leaving, the composer said to him: "However, leave
your paper with me." The following day the
musician came to the poet with the whole orches-

tration finished; he had spent the entire night composing it.

Immediately Father Richard mobilized teachers, seminarians and singers; they began rehearsing at once. On April 30, 1866, when the statue of Blessed Frances was carried in procession to the ducal château, three hundred musicians, arranged on the great staircase that leads to the ramparts, filled the court of honor with the marvelous, new cantata. Under the protection of the holy Duchess, the poet and the composer became the best of friends and have remained so. This cantata is sung every year in the preparatory seminary of Couëts on the feast day of Blessed Frances.

In his retirement at Talence, Bishop Jaquemet, no longer able to perform most of his episcopal functions, thought of asking of the imperial government that he be given a coadjutor. Father Richard seemed to him designated by Providence to fill this office. The Bishop thought he would find comfort in placing his diocese into hands so trustworthy. Without Father Richard's knowledge, he entrusted the plan to his secretary, Father de la Guibourgère, then to Archbishop Guibert, his metropolitan. The latter received this communication with joy. He said: "If needs be, I will myself write to the nuncio and to the Holy Father. On the part of Rome, no obstacle is to be feared."

At Paris everything seemed at first to go satisfactorily. But in high places they were not sure of Canon Richard's influence; they knew that worldly honors did not affect him and that he would show himself in all circumstances the zealous defender of the interests of the Church. Soon the answer came to Nantes, polite but unfavorable, from the Minister of Worship. Bishop Jaquemet was pained and did not hide his chagrin from Father Richard, who thus learned for the first time of the steps that had been taken in his regard. But the Bishop's attitude was altogether above human considerations. He wished to fulfill his duty, however painful to himself personally. He said: "Father Richard ought to be a bishop; the welfare of the Church requires it. Since they are not willing that he be bishop of Nantes, he must be raised to another see."

Unable to go to Rome in 1867 for the solemn anniversary of the martyrdom of St. Peter, Bishop Jaquemet wrote to Pius IX: "I will make up for my absence by sending Father Richard, my vicar general, whom Your Holiness has already deigned to receive several times with extreme kindness."

Reaching Rome at the beginning of June, Fa-

ther Richard was soon received in audience by the
Holy Father. During the whole month he kept up
a daily correspondence with his Bishop, who wrote
to him as follows:

> I follow you in thought and affection and prayer. I
> cannot tell you how much I was touched at your news
> and at the last marks of friendship at your departure,
> and how greatly I cherish that unalterable devotion to
> my poor suffering person. God will repay you. . . .
> While I am laboring to send you from me so that I may
> give you to another Church, I am performing the most
> heroic act of my life. This separation will be a foretaste
> of death for me. But neither of us must recoil before the
> sacrifices that God may ask of us.

On June 29 the memorable centenary of St. Peter's martyrdom was celebrated in Rome. The ceremonies in the basilica of St. Peter lasted from seven
o'clock in the morning until one o'clock in the
afternoon. The voice of the aged Pontiff, who was
now seventy-five years old, was as strong as ever.
The whole centennial celebration gave Father
Richard an impression of calmness and confidence
in the midst of the trials of the Church.

He transmitted to the Holy Father the generous
offerings of the diocese of Nantes for the main-
tenance of the papal zouaves. Seventy-two soldiers
from Nantes were thus supported at their expense.

For two years more the vicar general continued

his ceaseless labors at Nantes and wherever his ministry called him. All the pious works of Nantes were dear to him. But he was particularly mindful of that which was the firstfruits of his priesthood, the work of Our Lady of Joys. At the annual meeting in 1868, the occasion celebrated the return of the director, Father Peigné, who for some time had been chaplain in the papal army. Said Father Richard:

I see from the program that the meeting is to close with the *Magnificat*. Let me use this word to express what we all feel. We have seen and heard magnificent things, for which we must give praise to God. *Magnificat*. Let praise be given to the directors of this excellent work and to these dear boys and to these good young men and these worthy gentlemen who do it so much honor. *Magnificat*.

The Bishop's strength continued to decline. About the middle of November, 1869, his condition grew suddenly worse. He realized that the hour was approaching when he would leave this world. For some time past he had the oil of the infirm kept there at his country house so that, in case of a sudden crisis, he might not be deprived of extreme unction. But in prolonged diseases of the lungs, when life slowly ebbs away and when the patient's condition seems hardly to change from day to day, the patient himself does not easily appreciate when the hour has come for him to receive the sacraments. The Bishop relied on those about him to give him timely warning. The episcopal family surrounded him with tender devotion. During the night Fathers Vincent and de la Guibourgère watched at his bedside until one o'clock. Their places were taken by the Bishop's valet and Father Richard who, until morning, took care of the patient and gave him the help of his prayers.

Bishop Jaquemet died on December 9. The cathedral chapter named Father Richard and Father Laborde as capitular vicars. Father Richard assumed the entire administration of the diocese until the appointment of the new bishop.

The choice of Bishop Jaquemet's successor gave rise to some strife in the diocese of Nantes. A number of priests and laymen favored a certain priest who was eminent because of his personal worth and virtues, Father Fournier. Born in the parish of St. Nicholas, he had been curate and then pastor there and had spent himself generously for the construction of the marvelous basilica. But, as no one is a prophet in his own country, this candidacy had also adversaries. Unrestrained polemics arose on various sides. Canon Richard, always moved by supernatural motives, thought that, in the circumstances, the welfare of the diocese would be better served by the appointment of some priest outside of Nantes who would thus be above all parties. He therefore opposed the candidacy of Father Fournier, against whom he had no personal animosity at all, as the future would show. But Father Fournier's party triumphed. When the appointment became official, Father Richard offered his homage to the bishop-elect, frankly telling him: "I will not hide from you that I opposed your appointment conscientiously and canonically as strongly as I could." "Oh, my good Father Richard," replied the new bishop, "I know that you are a conscientious man."

Out of delicacy, Canon Richard withdrew from the diocesan office. We can but regret that Bishop Fournier did not retain the services of this valuable auxiliary for the diocesan administration. The former vicar general suffered from the trial, but never did he utter the slightest complaint or criticism. He never made any unfavorable allusion to it, but accepted it all with his habitual submission to the divine will, which he loved above all things. When later he himself was appointed bishop of Belley, he showed his greatness of soul by choosing as his consecrator, to everyone's astonishment and edification, the bishop of Nantes, Bishop Fournier.

CHAPTER VIII

Episcopal Appointment

UPON leaving the diocesan office, Father Richard along with Father Vincent, former secretary of Bishop Jaquemet, retired to a modest apartment. Thus he lived not far from his beloved cathedral and quite near his family. This time of trial from the hand of Providence was a preparation for the burden of the episcopacy. Bishop Colet of Luçon, knowing Father Richard's worth, offered him the title and position of vicar general. But Father Richard, not wishing to leave Nantes, accepted merely the title of honorary vicar general of Luçon.

Being no longer occupied with diocesan affairs, he consecrated all his hours to the service of the afflicted. He sought out the sick and infirm and showered his help and consolation upon them. His door was always open to those who were in need of counsel, of alms, or of comfort. His visitors were numerous, even too numerous to suit the taste of Frances Garreau, the devoted servant who along with her husband served Father Richard. The good woman was born at la Vergne. She worried about her master's delicate constitution. One day when she saw him return from his charitable visits somewhat paler and more worn than usual, she persuaded him to give orders that no callers should be admitted that evening. Scarcely had Father Richard retired, when someone came to the door. "Monsieur is not at home," Frances said without hesitation. But the doorbell disturbed the priest's rest. He ran into the hall and called out: "I am home for you, my friend." "It is not worth the trouble to lie," the servant exclaimed in despair; "they will end by killing him."

Father Richard's whole income passed through his hands into those of the poor. He gave not only his income in money, but even his income in kind. To the neediest spinners and weavers of Boussay he gave the flax harvested on his lands; and the white linen, even before it was taken off the loom, was promised to the poor.

The good priest, always ready to help others, was altogether indifferent about his own clothes. His servant said to him one day:

"I know of a wretchedly poor man who has not a single shirt fit to wear. Will you be so good as to help him?"

"Certainly," replied the charitable master; "how many shirts does he need?"

"I think it would be well to give him a good supply. Who knows when he will be able to get any more?"

"Very well. Cotton shirts, I suppose. They are cheaper."

"Cotton? That would do, of course. But this man has never worn any but linen shirts."

"Well, the good fellow must not change his habits. Get linen ones. I will pay for them."

The new shirts were put in the clothespress of "Monsieur Francis."

Father Richard continued to be the confessor of the Italians of Nantes and of many others who sought his wise spiritual guidance. He also continued to be active in the work of the Society of Christian Fathers which he founded while he was vicar general. In his retirement he did not forget his little native parish. On October 2, 1870, at Boussay he blessed the house of the Catholic school for girls. After Vespers the Rosary procession, following the new street opened at his expense, proceeded to the house. The ceremony was conducted according to the Roman Ritual. Then a little girl, in the name of the parish, thanked their benefactor because he had by many sacrifices provided a building for the religious instruction of the present generation and of generations to come.

A smallpox epidemic broke out at Nantes among the soldiers and then it attacked fifteen Christian Brothers who were acting as nurses. Some of them recovered quickly, but two of them contracted the black smallpox. The older one died in a few days. The other, Brother Désir, a Vendean twenty years old, hovered between life and death for six months. Only two brother nurses remained in touch with the unfortunate fellow, whose condition was horrible. Following the smallpox, a decomposition set in, and the flesh fell off in shreds. Several times a day his bed and his linen had to be changed. The priest who came to give him extreme unction was so affected that he became ill in consequence.

Brother Camillus then thought to acquaint Father Richard with the situation of the young brother. "I thank you for coming to me," said Father Richard. "If I had known the condition of this little brother sooner, I would have hastened at once."

He came, as calm and collected as if in the choir of a cathedral. He spoke to the dying brother about God, about the merit of patient suffering, and applied to him the indulgence of a happy death. He came every day, sometimes twice or three times a day. Without any fear, without showing his repugnance, he took the poor patient in his arms while the bedding was being changed.

The month of March came, and the sick brother's condition did not improve. Several times Father Richard tried to give him Communion, but in vain. The community made a novena to St. Joseph. On March 19 Brother Désir was able to receive Communion for the first time in several months. The convalescence began.

When Father Richard was appointed bishop of Belley, the very next day he himself brought the news to his "poor little brother"; and a few weeks later the brother was able, with slow little steps, to go to the Bishop's house to greet the holy prelate, who was about to leave Nantes.

Bishop Guibert, who had become archbishop of Paris, knew the worth and the virtues of the former vicar general of Nantes. Consulted about the choice of new bishops, he thought at once of Father Richard for the vacant see at Belley. On October 18, 1871, a decree of the government confirmed this nomination. The humble priest was the only one surprised at his elevation to the episcopate. "I was entirely unaware that they were thinking of me for your diocese," he wrote to the vicar general of

Belley. "At my baptism I was given St. Francis de Sales as my patron saint. The thought that the will of God today places me in a double sense under his patronage, is most agreeable to me, and I hope it will sustain me under whatever burdens Providence may be pleased to place on me."

Not without some pangs did the bishop-elect quit Brittany. To a Carmelite sister of Nantes he wrote: "The good God has called me, as He did you, to make the sacrifice of my family and my native soil. We must abandon ourselves without reserve to His holy will." To another he wrote: "The good God has not judged me worthy to receive a vocation to the religious life, but He has placed on me the cross of the episcopate. Ask Him that I may bear it with courage and that I may fulfill its duties with love for His holy will."

To place his new life under the protection of the saints of France, Father Richard made various pilgrimages. From Poitier, where he went to visit the tomb of Radegondis, he wrote to his nephew:

Dear Charles, I have read with great pleasure your letter which brought me news of yourself, of Anthony, and of dear Albert. I have not abandoned my plan of spending a few days with you all at Bel-Air. It is one of the good resolutions which I count on carrying out before I depart for Belley.

In leaving Nantes, among the sacrifices that I will offer

to the good God I must certainly include the sacrifice of being so far from my family.

I count much on your prayers. You are too good a Christian to regard the episcopate according to the outward glory which the world attaches to it. You will understand that this heavy burden requires that he on whom it is laid by the divine will must be aided by the fervent prayers of those who love him.

At Tours, at the tomb of St. Martin, our pious pilgrim notices a brother of the Holy Family, whose motherhouse is at Belley. Greeting the brother, he said: "You are the first member of my diocese that I have met. With all my heart I give you an embrace while waiting to give you my first blessing." And he warmly embraced the good brother.

The people of Boussay sent the Bishop-elect an address of felicitation, to which he replied by a letter to the pastor:

I have received the address of the good parishioners of Boussay which you sent me. I beg you to thank them while waiting until I can do so in person. The feelings expressed in this address have gone to my heart. I am attached to the Boussay parish by the fondest memories of my childhood, and I am accustomed to regard its inhabitants as forming, in a way, part of my family. They showed much affection toward my father and mother.

I did not need any outward sign to recall the bonds which I have with the Boussay parish and, if I had been consulted, I would have advised precisely what has been done, namely, to devote to the construction of the

94

church and to the glory of the good God all that would have been offered to me.

I will keep and will take to Belley with me the address which bears names that are well known to me, that I love, and that will recall all those of the parish. From time to time I will read it over again, and there see, along with the names of other inhabitants, those of my family. Often I will ask of God that all these names be inscribed in heaven.

I have a desire, before leaving Nantes, to celebrate Mass again in the Boussay church for all the families of the parish. I hope that our Lord will grant me this consolation.

The clergy of Belley wished to have the consecration of their bishop take place in their cathedral. Although touched by this attention, Bishop Richard was unable to yield to the request. To the vicar general, Father Buyat, he wrote:

This thought would be in conformity with the affection that I already feel for the diocese, but the ceremony has to take place in Paris. I have asked Archbishop Guibert, our former metropolitan, to give me the episcopal consecration. He has always been a father to me, the close and devoted friend of Bishop Jaquemet. I could not think of anyone but him as consecrating prelate, and I could not think of asking him to perform the ceremony outside of Paris. I am the one who should go to him.

Bishop Richard was preconized in a consistory of December 20. Immediately the cathedral chapter of Nantes hastened to pay its respects to the new bishop. He replied to the felicitations of the chapter by a few simple and cordial words.

Before leaving the diocese, Bishop Richard wished to give a pledge of affection to his fellow citizens by offering them the book of the *Saints of the Church of Nantes,* which he had just written. Modestly he endeavored to refer the honor to Bishop Jaquemet. In his preface he says:

> The book which we offer to the faithful of the Church of Nantes is one of Bishop Jaquemet's last inspirations. He was not satisfied with assuring and developing the liturgical cult of our saints. He wished the faithful to have in their hands a book that would teach them to know these saints, to love them, and to invoke them. He wished their history to have its place in Christian families, among the domestic souvenirs. This is the thought we have attempted to realize.

In a simple and practical style, the author sketches one after the other the lives of St. Amandus, St. Secondel, the two brothers, holy martyrs, Donatian and Rogatian, known by the name of "the children of Nantes," St. Similianus, St. Hervé, St. Gohard, St. Felix, St. Paquier, St. Frizard, St. Victor, St. Clare, St. Ursula and her companions, St. Benedict of Masérac, St. Vitalis, St. Martin of Vertou, St. Hermeland, Blessed Frances d'Amboise, and Blessed Grignon de Montfort.

With minute care, Bishop Richard put in order all his affairs at Nantes. The lot of his poor could not leave him indifferent. One friendly family offered to adopt one of his numerous clients. An excellent and venerable lady, who had greatly aided him in his works, asked him to leave her a souvenir before his departure. "Very gladly," he said; "I will think about it." A few days later she received a letter from the new Bishop, leaving her what he regarded as among his most precious possessions, three poor families to be nourished. In this manner he tried to distribute all the afflicted families whose care had been his concern. The baker who supplied the bread to Father Richard's poor received instructions to continue to furnish bread for a sum of 5,000 francs, but in the name of Bishop Fournier, bishop of Nantes. This touch of exquisite delicacy illustrates Bishop Richard's character.

For his coat of arms the new prelate might have taken a family armorial blazonry. But he preferred to make it entirely ecclesiastical. Bishop Jaquemet had adopted for his coat of arms that of the chapter of Nantes, merely adding a cross. Bishop Richard followed this idea in part. He took the lamb of St. John, such as it appears on the great seal of the chapter. To this he added three Breton ermines. For his device he took the motto of the Blessed

Duchess: Do all things that God may be better loved.

As we have already said, Bishop Richard wished to visit his parish of Boussay before going away. On January 18, 1872, he came there and solemnly blessed the cornerstone of the new church. A numerous escort of horsemen met him at the boundary of the parish, under the leadership of his grand-nephew George Pellerin de la Vergne. The Bishop was soon surrounded by the people of the neighboring villages. A bonfire was in readiness. As soon as he lighted it, the crowd shouted, "Long live the Bishop." Thus for the first time this cry greeted his ears in his familiar country. Pious mothers held up their infants to him, and all along the route was repeated the cry of "Long live the Bishop." To this he replied: "Long live Pius IX." At a little distance from the town the solemn reception took place. The priests of the parish and of the vicinity, the mayor, the town counselors, the members of the parish fabrique, the Society of Mutual Assurance, the school children, the notables of the parish, and a large throng of people came to pay their respects to Bishop Richard. After a few appropriate words by the president of the Society of Mutual Assurance, the procession passed through the streets of the town which, in spite of the season, presented an air of festivity, and reached the parish church. Bishop Richard then said Mass.

From the address of the pastor, Father Mérel, we quote the following lines:

We have the proof of your love for us in the continual exercise of your charity in the relief of the poor among us; in all the works inspired, encouraged, and sustained by your zeal for the glory of God and the spiritual welfare of the parish. We have proof of it especially in the sacrifices you have made to enable us to erect a temple to the God of heaven who deigns to dwell among us. The cornerstone which you are about to bless will be a stone of testimony. When another generation succeeds the generation that is witness of your virtue and your works, in thirty years, in fifty years, in a century, some father bringing his son into this church to pray, will say to him: "My son, see this stone. It was blessed on January 10, 1872, by one who was a boy of this parish. Sprung from one of the most honorable families of this region, he might have attained to a high position in the world. He became a priest, had an important place in the administration of the diocese of Nantes for more than twenty years. The good God made him a bishop, and he went off far from here to govern a diocese. This boy, this priest, this bishop, was called Francis Marie Benjamin Richard. Do not forget him, my son. Pass his name on to those who come after you." May Bishop Richard ever live in the hearts of the people.

In the procession which then went to the ceremony of the blessing of the cornerstone were seven priests and a deacon who were boys of the Boussay parish. The Bishop-elect of Belley blessed the foundations of the new church. The ceremony concluded by the singing of the *Te Deum*. Then Bishop Richard, after receiving the good wishes of the clergy, announced the date of his consecration as February 11.

He arrived at the Seminary of St. Sulpice three weeks before his consecration. When receiving the Nantes seminarians, he said to them:

> Pray for the poor Bishop of Belley. I have only three weeks before my consecration. In the meantime I shall have numerous matters to attend to. But I am determined to reserve the last ten days for myself. During that time I wish no one to speak to me about my consecration or about anything else except about the good God. Everything else must be attended to before that. Between now and then I shall do all I can in preparation for my retreat.

In fact, during those days which he called a time of preparation for his retreat, he regularly spent two or three hours in adoration before the Blessed Sacrament.

At the Seminary of St. Sulpice they had the custom of giving dinner every day to twelve poor families. Seven deacons took turns in distributing the food. Bishop Richard, when he was a seminarian, was one of these seven. Now, on the eve of his consecration, after dinner, instead of going directly to his room, he went to the place where the poor were served. He asked the deacon there present to yield his place to him. Then he put on the white apron and handed out the food. While speaking to them about God and distributing generous alms to them, he kept looking at a certain old man. He thought he recognized him.

"Where have we met before?" he asked him.

"I used to come here in your day, Bishop," the old man answered.

"Yes, indeed. Now I remember you, my friend."

Then, after asking them all to pray for him, he said: "I should be glad to give you all one of my first blessings here tomorrow. But this I cannot do because I shall not return to the seminary after my consecration. But I promise that I will send you my blessing which I shall be unable to bring personally."

This promise he kept. At the close of the consecration ceremonies, the assisting seminarians, as soon as they returned to the sacristy, gathered around the Bishop to receive his first blessing. While they were still kneeling around him, he told the chief almoner of the poor to stand up and come to him. Then he took from his pocket a rather large box which he had been carrying on his person since early morning. It was filled with crucifixes

101

and medals, which he then blessed and handed to the seminarian for distribution to the poor, saying: "Tell my dear poor people that I love them and that I bless them with all my heart." This was indeed one of his first blessings. He had not yet seen his family, who were then waiting for him. Thus did Bishop Richard begin his episcopate.

He wished his consecration to take place with the utmost simplicity and invited only his closest friends. He had chosen for the purpose the chapel of St. Thomas of Villanova, where there was a statue of the Blessed Virgin before which his patron, St. Francis de Sales, had obtained a great grace. But, on account of the smallness of the chapel, this plan had to be abandoned. The ceremony took place in the chapel of the Madames of the Sacred Heart.

Three days later Bishop Richard left for Belley.

CHAPTER IX

Bishop of Belley

(1872 to 1875)

IMMEDIATELY upon taking possession of the episcopal see of Belley, Bishop Richard issued his first pastoral letter, which breathes his gentle spirit. But we must be satisfied with quoting a few passages from it.

The portion which the Lord has bestowed on us is a portion of predilection, and we already love our inheritance, so rich with divine graces. On your blessed soil we will try to follow the footsteps of your saints, of your great bishop of the Middle Ages, St. Anthelmus, who left the sweetness of solitude to devote himself to the salvation of souls. At the threshold of modern times, you saw the gentle figure of the holy bishop of Geneva, St. Francis de Sales, our patron. Our heart is thrilled when we think that, in spite of our unworthiness, we are called to harvest a part of his heritage. Henceforth we will love him the more since he is now doubly our father and we beseech him ever to rule over the diocese which was his and that of his friend, the great servant of the poor, St. Vincent de Paul, who also marked his passage in your country and left his imprint here. In your country the succession of saints has been uninterrupted. In our midst is the tomb of the Curé of Ars. One of our chief cares will be to labor for advancing the day when the Church will permit us to honor with public worship that humble priest, whose life has recalled to our days the marvels of the ages of faith.

A few days later, on the first Sunday of Lent, Bishop Richard officiated pontifically in his episcopal city. The church was filled to overflowing. The whole population rejoiced, and their veneration for the new Bishop was unbounded. The reason for this feeling was that they had found a saint. The expression of this feeling was on every lip and in various forms; but most frequently it was expressed thus: "We have the Curé become a bishop." Bishop Richard was an amiable saint, like his patron St. Francis de Sales.

All the streets of Belley were decorated: flags and penants by the thousand. Every last house showed some sort of festive adornment. In the evening the whole city sparkled with lights.

Seven o'clock came. The Bishop appeared. The whole city seemed to be waiting for him in the great court of the episcopal palace. He was greeted with the fanfare of the college; the crowd applauded. The good Bishop, accompanied by his chapter, passed through the streets of the city, as in a tri-

umphal procession. Now the whole city was aflame.
All classes took part in this impressive demonstra-
tion. The good prelate advanced slowly, the whole
population being his escort, pressing about him,
looking at him. When he stopped, they stopped;
when he went ahead, they went ahead. Where he
was, there was the whole town; where he was not,
the town was deserted. The people were drawn by
the magnetism of holiness.

To the service of the Church of Belley, Bishop
Richard brought the same zeal and tireless devotion he had shown in his twenty years at Nantes.
Soon the various good works of his diocese became
familiar to him, and his pastoral ministry brought
him personally to every part of the territory under
his jurisdiction.

He had frequent occasion to go to Bourg, the
most important city of his diocese. From there a
short journey brought him to the seminary at Brou,
where he often went for retreats and ordinations.
His very presence was an edification. During one
of his visits to the seminary, one evening the superior was making his visit to the Blessed Sacrament in a retired corner of the chapel. Nightfall
had come and the chapel was now dark. Bishop
Richard entered the chapel, carrying a candle and
supposing, of course, that he was quite alone with

our Lord. After an adoration before the altar, he arose, put the candle on a corner of the altar, and then, standing, began to recite his breviary, giving free rein to the outpourings of his piety. Every now and then his eyes were raised to the door of the tabernacle, full of confidence and love. When certain words of the office aroused particular feeling, then his voice took on a still greater unction and his eyes shone more brightly.

The superior realized that, if his presence should be betrayed, the Bishop's humility would be offended. For the space of a full hour he succeeded in remaining perfectly still. When at last the Bishop withdrew, the superior fell to his knees and thanked God for having shown him the transports of a saint at prayer.

As at Nantes, Bishop Richard bestowed his prodigal care on the schools and religious houses of the diocese. One after the other, he visited the Trappists, the Carthusians, the Brothers of the Holy Family, and the Brothers of the Cross of Jesus who are engaged in the education of the young.

One day every week found him at the house of the Marist Fathers to go to confession. If some novices were already waiting in his confessor's anteroom, he refused to go in ahead of them, and humbly waited for his turn.

All the religious communities in his diocese were objects of his benevolence. We mention specifically the following: the Congregation of St. Joseph, the Daughters of St. Bernard, the Dominicans, the Ursulines, the Visitation nuns, the Marist Sisters, the Sisters of the Cross, the Sisters of St. Martha and St. Charles, the Daughters of Charity, and the Servants of Mary. Everywhere he brought the example of his amiable virtues and especially of that deep humility which worldly honors could not lessen.

In the first months of his episcopacy, Bishop Richard encouraged the founding of a religious weekly paper at Belley. It was published under the title of *Messager du Dimanche* ("Sunday Visitor"). In the first number appears a greeting from the Bishop, from which we quote the following lines:

Our little *Messager du Dimanche* is about to knock at the door of Christian families. We hope that its very name will give it a welcome. It will recall a man loved and venerated by everyone in the diocese of Belley, "our saint," the Curé of Ars. With the wonderful insight of the saints, he understood the great social plague of our day and the remedy needed to cure it. May the *Messager du Dimanche* be the continuation of his labor and may it repeat to all each week the fatherly words which the Venerable Father Vianney addressed to his parishioners: "Sunday is something that belongs to the good God, it is His, the Lord's Day. A day which you steal from the Lord will not profit you."

Bishop Richard's care was to increase the Christian life about him and to reanimate its essential practices. Among these is first of all the sanctification of Sunday and the Sunday rest. He made these the subject of his Lenten pastoral letter in 1873. He knew that Lyons had an association which was carrying on a strife against the violation of the Sunday. He wished to institute a similar work at Belley, following the same regulations.

The confirmation circuit occupied a considerable portion of the springtime. A carefully prepared itinerary brought him from parish to parish and combined the apostolic life with the quiet recollection of the humble parish rectory. Bishop Richard always showed becoming deference for the prominent families of the district and was grateful for their cooperation in good works. But he had no liking for social receptions, which can easily consume time that might be devoted to the parish visitation.

The exchange of courtesies with the civil authorities, who at that time showed themselves respectful of episcopal authority, did indeed claim a place in the program of his strenuous days. And he was graciously ready to lend himself to these exigencies. Especially at Bourg numerous contacts with the civil authorities occurred. At the traditional festival of the city, the prefect and all the officials, as well as the military officers, took part in the procession.

At times the good Bishop attended the military Mass which was celebrated every Sunday in the chapel of the Lycée and which was attended by a large number of officers. He also visited the camp at Vallebonne and took an interest in all the services of that military establishment and likewise in the life of the soldiers.

But for Bishop Richard the solemn civic ceremonies were merely obligations of his office. His exquisite courtesy rendered them easy and pleasant, but without absorbing his attention.

Above all else he was a man of the Church, and he was particularly attracted by the religious ceremonies. The consecration of the church at Miribel, that of the church at Pont-d'Ain, were festivities that appealed to him, as also the blessing of the church bells at Trévoux. He gladly prolonged his visit to Gex, where the memory of St. Francis of Sales is to be found at every step. He was fond of looking for the signature of the great Bishop on the parish registers. When the duties of his episcopal office left him a little leisure, he found particular delight in following, in his diocese, the traces of the saints and in making pilgrimages to the spots where they lived. Thus he visited the spot where St. Rambert was martyred and the birthplace of Blessed Chanel.

He exercised his pious zeal in hastening the canonization of the Curé of Ars. On August 4, 1872, he celebrated at Ars the thirteenth anniversary of Father Vianney's death. On this occasion he wrote as follows to the faithful of the diocese:

Those of you who have made the pilgrimage know what a fragrance of holiness preserves these places made holy by the footsteps of the venerable priest. The simple rectory, his plain bedroom, where he lived and where he died, have remained in exactly the state in which he left them, a continual reflection of his mortified life and of his complete detachment from the things of earth. The unpretentiousness of his tomb continues the humility of his life and will do so until the day when the Church decrees him the honors of public worship.

Upon returning from his first journey to Rome as Bishop, he wrote:

One circumstance of my visit to Rome has a special interest for our country. There one of my first cares was to treat of the cause of the venerable servant of God, the Curé of Ars. God has heard your desires and mine. I was able to obtain and I have brought back with me the remissorial letters for starting the apostolic process of the beatification of the holy Curé. In a few days we shall, by virtue of the delegation of the Holy See, call together the ecclesiastical tribunal which, in the name of the Pope and by his authority, will gather information about the heroic virtues of the servant of God.

This will be a great joy for all of us. The glorification of the saints is the common joy of Christian peoples. When the fourth of August comes, the anniversary of the precious death of Father Vianney, we shall gather in larger numbers than ever before at the humble tomb, praying the Lord to crown our efforts with success and to bestow His abundant blessings upon the great Pontiff who spoke to me warmly about the venerable priest so much beloved by our people.

Bishop Richard came to Belley in the days immediately following the Franco-German War. The National Assembly, to which the destinies of the country were entrusted, felt the need of heavenly assistance and asked public prayers for France. The Bishop of Belley rejoiced at this national homage to the sovereign Master and was at pains to give these public prayers all the outward solemnity that befitted them.

His heart was grieved at the religious persecution that desolated the Catholics of Switzerland. When Bishop Mermillod, the vicar apostolic of

Geneva, was unjustly exiled by the civil authorities, Bishop Richard gave him the most fraternal welcome. A fondness for each other united the two prelates who at Nantes had celebrated together the glories of the Blessed Frances d'Amboise. Not long afterward Bishop Lechat of Bâle and the priests of the Bernese Jura, likewise exiled on account of their loyalty to the Holy See, found the same sympathy with Bishop Richard.

Without stint the Bishop of Belley gave his time and strength to his beloved diocese. He was rarely absent. His *ad limina* visit to Rome, a few journeys to Paray-le-Monial, Lourdes, and Annecy, a few visits to Paris and Nantes, a short visit to Lyons and to Autun for a religious ceremony, sum up the hours snatched from his pastoral life. But his health was again threatened by the harsh climate and the excess of work. Two or three times he was obliged to seek a little rest and medical care. In July, 1873, his doctors advised a season at Eaux-Bonnes.

Even though absorbed by the concerns of his diocese, Bishop Richard could not forget those of Nantes. His soul was too lofty for his new affections to lessen the old. For the course of Lenten sermons in the Belley cathedral, he invited Father Jubineau, superior of the diocesan missioners of Nantes.

At the time of the first pilgrimages organized for Lourdes, some bands of men in the pay of the freemasons heaped insults and even blows on the peaceful pilgrims as they were returning to Brittany. Bishop Richard wrote:

How often I have thought of you during the Lourdes pilgrimage and during the days that followed! The people of Nantes were admirable, and did not lack glorious manifestations of their faith, not even insults suffered for the name of our Lord Jesus Christ and the Blessed Virgin. The Bishop of Nantes must have been greatly consoled by the enthusiasm of the people, who so well responded to his appeal. If you have occasion to see him, please offer him my respects and tell him how much I have rejoiced with him at the piety and strength of the sturdy people of Nantes.

Bishop Richard's fondness for his family never diminished. He kept up an active correspondence with them, sharing their joys and their sorrows. During a pastoral visit to Bourg, he learned that the young son of his nephew Charles had just been accidentally shot and that his life was in danger. At once he wrote, asking for details of the accident and of the condition of the little sufferer. Every day, during the many months of Albert's recovery, he continued to remember him in his prayers to the Blessed Virgin and to the Curé of Ars. The very day when he said Mass at Ars for

Albert, the lead shots began coming out of the wound.

When the time for Albert's first Communion arrived, his granduncle wrote him as follows:

You have started your retreat. During these days when you are preparing for your first Communion and your confirmation, I will be thinking of you often and will pray for you. I had the consolation of giving you baptism on a feast day of the Blessed Virgin, and this good mother has taken you under her protection. Last year she watched over you after the terrible accident you had. I hope she will protect you always until some day she will lead you into heaven. May our Lord Jesus Christ remain your best friend during your whole life. I bless you along with your good parents.

As often as circumstances permitted, he used to gather about him his nephews and nieces, his grandnephews, and even his great-grandnephews. On January 4, 1873, he wrote:

"I am going to make my retreat in Paris at the end of the month. This circumstance will enable me to gratify Marie's wish and go to Laval to baptize her little daughter. Probably I will go on February 1, remain the next day, and leave on the third. I have very little time to myself before beginning my pastoral visitations on February 9. Be so good as to come to Laval and make the journey with Leonide."

Bishop Richard's physical condition was such that his doctor insisted he should spend another season at Eaux-Bonnes, that is, until the end of July. He then planned a short visit to his Echasserie estate to see his oldest nephew Louis Pellerin de la Vergne, who was in poor health. He wrote:

"Probably I shall again go to Lourdes, which I also visited on my way here. Then I will stop at Auch to see Bishop de Langalerie, my venerable predecessor; give a day to the family of Bishop Jaquemet at Bordeaux; make a little visit to the Bishop of Luçon, and reach l'Echasserie, where I shall stay from August 5 to 7.

"I can scarcely wait to see Louis. I confess that I am more and more anxious about him. The thought of visiting him is one of the great reasons for my journey."

But a few days later the Bishop of Belley conducted to his last resting place him whom he regarded as a brother. He felt the loss keenly. Louis' name was often repeated in his prayers and in his letters. Not long after this, he wrote from Nancy:

I have come here to attend a meeting of the bishops of the Besançon province. I do not forget Louis, for whom I pray every day and often offer up the sacrifice of the Mass.

Three Scripture texts come to my mind, from which you

may choose for an inscription on his tombstone. *Beati mortui qui in Domino moriuntur* ("Blessed are they who die in the Lord"); this is the text you chose for your father's tombstone. *Non habemus hic manentem civitatem, sed futuram inquirimus* ("We have not here a lasting city, but seek one that is to come"). This text would recall that Louis offered to the good God the sacrifice of the house which he had built on earth and prepared in a Christian manner to obtain the abode of eternity. This would be appropriate for a tomb at the family house and would indicate that those who inhabit that house wish, like him who built it, to seek especially the heavenly home. The third text expresses the consolation that Christian families find in the hopes of the faith and that Louis has left us by his Christian death: *Non contristamini sicut et coeteri qui spem non habent* ("Be not sad as those who have no hope").

I often recall the days we spent together at la Vergne and l'Echasserie. Those places, where we passed our boyhood, are filled with Christian memories for us. Our good parents, who brought us up there, now wait for us in heaven. All these thoughts are good for our soul and encourage us to lead a Christian life.

In the early summer of that year, after two months of pastoral visitations, Bishop Richard needed to seek a little rest. This he took at the house of the diocesan missioners at Pont-d'Ain. The building, a former château of the dukes of Savoy, was located in a charming solitude in a secondary chain of the Jura mountains.

During his visit to la Vergne in August, 1873,

Bishop Richard celebrated, in the place of his birth, the patronal feast of St. Radegunda and in the evening took part in the customary procession of the relics. He was accompanied by his vicar general, Father Bertrand, and by Fathers Laborde, Picaud, and Vincent, who had been his companions in the bishop's residence at Nantes and who enjoyed talking over old times with him.

A few months later, when he made his *ad limina* visit to Rome, he presented to Pius IX, in the name of the Boussay parish, the address which had been confided to him for the purpose. It said:

"Most Holy Father, the priests and faithful of the parish of Boussay, diocese of Nantes, the birthplace of Bishop Richard of Belley, profiting by his presence in Rome, express to Your Holiness their feelings of filial veneration and their grief at the persecutions directed against the august person of the Vicar of Jesus Christ.

"The people of Boussay, encouraged and sustained by Bishop Richard, have now rebuilt their parish church. They and the priests of the parish would be greatly encouraged to continue their sacrifices and would consider it a precious memory if Your Holiness would deign to grant them the apostolic blessing."

The petition bore seven hundred signatures.

The Holy Father replied with his own hand, writing: *Benedicat vos Deus et dirigat vos in omnibus viis suis. P. Pius IX* ("May God bless you and direct you in all His ways").

CHAPTER X

Coadjutor of Cardinal Guibert

FEELING his strength becoming enfeebled, the venerable archbishop of Paris, Cardinal Guibert, resolved to associate the Bishop of Belley in his office, with the right of succession. Early in 1875 he wrote to Bishop Richard as follows:

"I need near me a bishop like you. I know you; you seek only the glory of God and you are animated only by the love of souls. Worldly considerations have no hold on you, and honors do not affect you."

Bishop Richard's modesty took fright at the honor offered him. For three years he declined the pressing solicitations of Cardinal Guibert who, at the end of arguments, based his appeal on the example of his predecessors: Bishops Affre, Sibour, and Darboy, who had been expiatory victims of France. He said: "A person may refuse a bishopric, an archbishopric, but not martyrdom." The Holy

119

Father supported his insistent pleas. Bishop Richard no longer refused, "notwithstanding the sorrow he might experience at leaving the see of Belley and the dread he felt at the thought of assuming charge of the diocese of Paris."

On May 8 the Minister of Worship made the official announcement of the nomination of the coadjutor. Shortly afterward the news reached Belley, spreading grief on all sides. From all directions came testimonials of regret and of respectful attachment for the beloved pastor. While he was at the Seminary at Brou, he received a visit from M. Villefranche, author of the *Life of Pius IX,* who spoke to him of his appointment as coadjutor of Paris as a foreseen advancement. Bishop Richard replied by showing the letter of Cardinal Guibert, which was an urgent appeal, not to honors, but to devotion.

Bishop Mermillod wrote to him, saying:

A visit to the diocese of Belley without you there will be a real exile for me. In spite of my regrets, I congratulate the Church, France, and Paris on the mission of sacrifice that is entrusted to you. It is not above your heart and your virtues. I have begged St. Francis de Sales and the venerable Curé of Ars to spare us this separation. But God knows how to choose His pontiffs and to place them in their right place in His vineyard. I suffer from this decision, which I quite understand on the part of the Cardinal of Paris and of the Supreme Pontiff. Sacrifice and obedience always find you ready. But I was your brother, your son, a member of your family, and I belonged to your heart. You will pardon me for this lament of my respectful affection. May St. Denis keep you for the Church, for France, for those who love and venerate you. I know how much you have resisted, but you cannot escape the chalice which two angels, those of Paris and of Rome, present to you for the glory of the Master.

On July 30, at four o'clock in the afternoon, Bishop Richard left the episcopal city. After receiving the farewells of his cathedral chapter, he perceived in the courtyard of the palace the faithful who had come in crowds. A deep emotion filled their hearts. The former Bishop of Belley could not hold back his tears and again blessed those about him. He went to the tomb of the humble Curé of Ars to seek the recollection which was always dear to his soul. There he received, August 5, a pilgrimage from Paris. Then, before finally going away, he addressed a last blessing to the people of the Belley diocese.

On August 7, he reached Paris, and six days later, the feast of St. Radegunda, he was solemnly installed at Notre Dame in his new office, with the title of archbishop of Larissa.

Without taking any respite from labor, Archbishop Richard at once began his laborious ministry. "If you follow me in my peregrinations," he wrote to his nephew, "I am often with you and the whole family in thought and especially in my prayers. Probably you know that I have been at Paris since the 7th of August. These first three weeks have passed amid occupations and visits that are the necessary consequence of an appointment to a new post. I am not yet completely installed; my library is not yet in order."

On the second floor of a house on rue de Grenelle, the coadjutor occupied a modest apartment of three or four rooms which, by its monastic simplicity and its rustic character, might remind Archbishop Richard of the old tower of the bishop's house at Nantes. Some books and a desk loaded with papers formed all the luxury of his lodgings. But the visitors who knocked at the door knew they would find with the Archbishop of Larissa the same benevolent welcome that people used to receive from the vicar general of Bishop Jaquemet. And to the interests of the Church of Paris he brought also the same conscientious zeal. The community life of the Archbishop's house quite agreed with his desires.

The Coadjutor's first visits were to the hospitals and the prisons. The priests' retreat brought him into touch with the clergy. Soon all the pastors and the directors of the various diocesan activities sought his counsel and his encouragement. The thickly populated parishes were for Archbishop Richard an object of particular attention, and the religious communities could likewise count on his unbounded devotion. This labor edified Cardinal Guibert but also made him anxious for his coadjutor, whose zeal took no account of the limits of human strength.

At the end of September the Archbishop of Larissa, who was at his Echasserie estate for a short rest, took advantage of his visit to bless the Boussay church, which had recently been completed. Three years before he had blessed the cornerstone. The whole countryside was in festive spirit. On October 2, 1875, the mile-long route to the church was decorated with triumphal arches, bonfires, and other festive signs.

After the ceremony at the church, the Archbishop went to la Vergne. Perhaps this was the occasion when, after dinner, he was surprised to find on the front steps two old soldiers, wearing bearskin hats and each carrying an axe on his shoulder. There they stood rigidly at attention, mounting guard in his honor. They may have been astonished that the prelate declined this military honor. The next day he blessed the new church and addressed the faithful, urging them to keep intact the faith handed down to them by their ancestors. At night-fall he mingled with the throng gathered before the Lourdes grotto to offer their homage to the Blessed Virgin.

One of the first projects for which Cardinal Guibert asked his coadjutor's collaboration was the building of the national basilica of the Sacred Heart. The laying of the cornerstone had taken place only a few days before Archbishop Richard's arrival in Paris. Until the end of his life he took an active part in the undertaking. While awaiting the completion of the great edifice on Montmartre, Cardinal Guibert (March 3, 1876) opened a provisional chapel where, the next day, Archbishop Richard celebrated Mass and where, on the following June 23, he officiated at the first feast of the Sacred Heart, a prelude to so many such feasts that followed.

The formation of the Catholic Institute occupied Archbishop Richard particularly. Two days before his installation as coadjutor, he was appointed president of the permanent commission, chosen to handle the practical problems of the young university. Along with Father d'Hulst, he became its most zealous protector. In 1877 he went to Rome, accompanied by Father Pelgé, the future bishop of Poitiers. Among the various affairs which he had to treat of with the Supreme Pontiff, those of the Catholic Institute were of the first importance. He reserved for himself the care of providing for the religious needs of the new foundation which, on November 7, 1878, opened its higher school of theology, to which was soon added the teaching of canon law, entrusted to an eminent Roman professor, the future Cardinal Gasparri.

Cardinal Guibert and his coadjutor had a high mutual regard for each other. The cordiality of the Cardinal's feelings is shown in the following extract from one of his letters.

I have just read in the newspaper about your celebration of the feast of St. Anne. On the morning of the consecration of the church, you had a torrential downpour of rain. Fortunately you did not have to take an active part in the ceremony. The consecrator who had to sprinkle the exterior of the church did not find his pluviale much protection. But I fear that the humidity may have retarded the cure of your bronchitis. You will give me a great pleasure by writing me a short note addressed to the archbishop's house at Aix, telling me the news about your health. I ask the good God to give you strength suited to present labors and those which are ahead.

When Archbishop Richard was called to Paris as coadjutor, the public authorities were still respectful toward Catholic institutions. But in 1880 began the religious war for the expulsion of the Jesuits of rue de Sèvres. Although Archbishop Richard gladly kept aloof from the political strifes, he always showed himself the fearless defender of the interests of the Church and seconded Cardinal Guibert's views with tireless zeal.

Whatever labors were demanding his attention, Archbishop Richard was always accessible to everybody. Whenever one of the servants at the archbishop's house took sick, he asked for the spiritual assistance of Archbishop Richard. Six or seven servants received from his hands the sacrament of extreme unction and received from him also a pious exhortation before leaving this world and appearing before God.

When the steward of his estates at Boussay became grievously ill, Archbishop Richard was kept informed about his condition. To his nephew he wrote as follows:

Thanks for the news about poor Esprit. Your letter confirms my intention of going to see him next Wednesday before I start out for Paris. I wish to bless him and bid him farewell before he leaves this world. I pray often for good Esprit. Ever since my boyhood I have been fond of him, who was so devoted to all of us. Please write to Josephine that she should send Esprit word of her coming

126

visit so that he will not be too much affected when he sees her. . . .

I have written a few kind lines to Esprit. I was happy to learn that he could go to church and receive Communion on the Sunday after our visit.

And again he wrote, after Esprit's death, saying:

I continue to pray for him. I will not forget his constant devotion to our family. It was largely to see him once more that I journeyed to Nantes in June. Our fondness for him will now show itself by our prayers. The truly Christian dispositions in which he died give us abundant hope that we shall see him in heaven.

On June 7, 1881, Archbishop Richard gave confirmation to the children of Ménilmontant. After the ceremony, Father Pisani, the director of the parish school, related that a boy who had smallpox received his first Communion that very morning on his sickbed. "I must go and confirm him," said the Archbishop. And at once he made his way to the poor attic. To the sick boy he administered the sacrament of strength and resignation, and thus bestowed on him and his mother the sweetest consolation. And he left his purse behind him with the poor family.

From his early years, Archbishop Richard was accustomed to spend himself in the service of souls. But often his physical strength gave way before his zeal and forced him to take a rest. In 1877, Father Laborde, appointed Bishop of Blois, chose the Archbishop of Larissa as his consecrator. But the latter was then very unwell and was thus prevented from even attending the ceremony. The former vicar general of Bishop Jaquemet would have been much pleased to consecrate his colleague and friend. A few weeks later he was able to write his family that convalescence was progressing and that he was now able to remain out of bed a great part of the day. Upon his doctors' advice that he should go as soon as possible to breathe his native air, he decided to go directly to l'Echasserie without stopping at Nantes. Whenever he went to Nantes, an endless stream of callers always came to see him, and his habitual kindness made him accessible to all.

In 1876 the people of Nantes proposed the name of the Archbishop in the senatorial elections. But the honors of this world had no attraction for him. He replied that the duties of a senator were incompatible with the ministry of a bishop in a diocese of 2,000,000 souls.

When Father Martin, a missioner belonging to the diocese of Nantes, was appointed bishop of the Marquesas Islands, Canon Robert, the director of the Propagation of the Faith Society in Nantes, at once sent the news to Archbishop Richard. The latter, wishing to give some souvenir to the new Bishop, wrote to Canon Robert: "I have only one ring besides the one I am wearing. I am happy to make him a present of it and I think the gift will please him."

Cardinal Guibert's old age had not prevented him from governing his diocese with firmness and from exercising an undisputed authority, without any part of the diocesan administration suffering, thanks to the activity and zeal of the coadjutor. In the spring of 1885 the Cardinal's health was seriously impaired, but he recovered from the attack. Again, however, he became increasingly weaker and died about a year later. The deceased prelate said in his will:

I recommend to my dear and respected coadjutor that he should not let himself be carried off by his zeal and that he care for his health, which is important for the good of the Church of Paris, especially in the times through which we are now passing. I recommend myself to his prayers, and I thank him for the active cooperation which he has given me in the last years of my episcopate.

Shortly before his death, Cardinal Guibert, testifying to the perfect understanding that existed between himself and his coadjutor, said: "During the ten years that we have been together, we never had a moment of disagreement."

Archbishop Richard throughout his life continued his interest in the parish of his boyhood and in the affairs of his friends of those early days. This interest remained particularly active toward his relatives. We add here a few instances by way of illustration.

Certain changes being carried out in the Boussay cemetery required the transfer of Archbishop Richard's family graves. From Paris he directed his nephew in the arrangements to be made for the new burial. As an inscription to be carved on the pedestal of the tombstone, he chose: "Do all things that God may be better loved." This was the motto he had adopted for his episcopal coat of arms. As he knew that his own remains would not be laid to rest in the Boussay cemetery, he thus provided a remembrance at the foot of the cross erected above the graves of his family.

He also arranged in advance the details for the ceremony of the transfer of the remains to the new graves. On the appointed day, after he had said a requiem Mass in the parish church, he went processionally to the cemetery as is customary on All Souls Day. There he blessed the new graves. Then

130

at the cemetery cross he gave the general absolution for all the deceased of the parish to show that his family was closely united with all the good families of Boussay and that, while praying for his relatives, he was praying also for theirs. Near the graves of his family were some other open graves. As he turned to these to pray for the souls of those whose remains were there, someone standing at his side said to him: "Monsignor, these are not the graves of your family." "My good friend," he replied, "they are our brothers in Christ."

A few weeks after this event, two priests from Nantes preached a mission at Boussay. Archbishop Richard wrote to the pastor that he was praying for the success of the mission, promising to celebrate a Mass especially for the people of Boussay, asking our Lord to preserve in their hearts the good fruits of the mission. He wrote further: "Whenever I visit you I am always glad to see that the good families keep their habits of faith and piety. May the good God grant us the grace to meet some day in heaven."

He himself bought a plot in the cemetery as a burying place for the Boussay pastors. In writing to the pastor on this occasion he reminded him that the memory of their good priests is held in benediction by the faithful. "This ought to encourage us to support the difficulties and sufferings that now burden us as those who preceded us supported their trials. May our Lord and His holy Mother bless you more and more in your ministry in that beloved parish of Boussay."

The care of the poor perpetually occupied Archbishop Richard's mind. Wherever he passed, the poor could appreciate his generosity. The poor of his native parish and its neighborhood were never forgotten. Writing to his nephew, he said:

My dear Charles, I wish to take up the question of the poor of Boussay. I used to leave to Esprit the actual arrangements according to my instructions. I wish now to send to you each year the sum which I have been accustomed to use for these good works of our old boyhood parish. I will indicate how I desire to have this sum employed and I leave to you the care of arranging each year the relief in food, clothing, and so forth. I know you love the people of Boussay. It seems to me that you will be glad to continue the traditions of our parents in bringing assistance to the poor.

To meet the demands of his many charities, Archbishop Richard reduced his personal expenses to what was strictly necessary. Any superfluous expense seemed to him to diminish the welfare of the poor. At la Vergne a room intended for his use whenever he visited there, was to be refurnished. But he insisted that the furniture should be very modest because, as he wrote, he could not forget that he had so many poor people around him.

Archbishop Richard was impelled by a desire to give pleasure to others. Upon receiving New Year's greetings from the children in the Sisters' school at Boussay, he sent them, as a New Year's gift, a beautiful oleograph picture of the Sacred Heart which had recently been given to him. He directed his nephew to have it framed at his expense.

CHAPTER XI

Archbishop of Paris

IN sending to the Minister of Worship the official notification of the death of Cardinal Guibert, the coadjutor for the first time signed himself, "Francis, Archbishop of Paris." The minister in his reply used the same title. Thus was refuted a rumor that certain members of the government were raising difficulties because they feared to find in Archbishop Richard a fearless defender of the interests of the Church. They hoped to remove him far from Paris by having the Pope appoint him a cardinal in Curia.

In the course of his eleven years as coadjutor, he had come to know the priests of the diocese, their names, their offices, and their special aptitudes. His previous experience at Nantes and at Belley, followed by these years in Paris, had prepared him to take direct personal charge of the administration of the Paris diocese.

The large study which he now occupied in the archbishop's house was lined with canonical and liturgical works and with collections of the decisions of the Holy See. His desk was piled with documents and correspondence. There he regularly began his day's work at eight o'clock in the morning, after his meditation and Mass. Each of the vicars general and the officers of the diocesan administration came to him there with urgent questions or with some official document to be signed. Archbishop Richard left off work only to visit the chapel or to make a hasty preparation for some ceremony. Besides the solemnities celebrated in the principal churches, there were few days that did not call him to some parish or religious community or some good work in the diocese.

The days that were free from these appointments were given partly to the reception of the priests and the faithful. It was the Archbishop's express wish that all his priests should have free access to him. Thus each of them could receive his directions, his counsel, and his encouragement.

The diverse affairs that had to be treated brought to him Catholics who were engaged in various good works, jurists, financiers, statesmen, business men. Whatever was the office or occupation of the person and whatever the nature of the interview,

Archbishop Richard listened with kindness and attention.

In the room adjoining his study he received persons of the world, without giving any evidence of being pressed by the work that was awaiting him at his desk, and always leaving an impression of a goodness that was not of earth.

Father Icard, the Archbishop's spiritual director, admired his zeal but somewhat regretted the amount of time thus taken from affairs of greater importance. He feared especially, he said, that the Archbishop would succumb to so many fatigues without rest. Therefore he expressed his opinion that the Archbishop would do well to restrict his interviews and not be so ready to receive every comer. Archbishop Richard listened to him without interruption; then, with a gentle smile, he simply replied: "My dear Father Superior, I have so little of the virtues of my holy patron, that, to resemble him in some way, I must at least have his faults. Your reproach is the very one that was made to St. Francis de Sales."

In spite of his absorbing occupations, the new Archbishop continued, apart from the confirmation tours, the regular visitation of the parishes. These were numerous: seventy in Paris, and seventy-three in the rest of his diocese. He knew them all and made sure of their proper administration by devoting two full days to the examination of each one. He overlooked no detail, giving practical advice on each point. And he always celebrated a requiem Mass for the deceased members of the parish that he was visiting.

The laicizing of the schools and hospitals was a painful blow to him. One of his first preoccupations as archbishop of Paris was to assure by collections the support of the hospital chaplains, whom the government refused to recognize and remunerate. Recalling the decision taken by Cardinal Guibert when confronted by this religious hostility, he also wished that the sick should not be deprived of spiritual help, lest any of those souls, for whom Christ died, should perish through his fault.

God brings good out of evil. At the side of the antireligious laws, the works of charity increased in number. "We are deeply moved," wrote the Archbishop, "at the thought of the charity which daily assumes every form in relieving the miseries of our immense Capital."

The Bishop of Nantes invited Archbishop Richard to bless the new church at Vallet. The invitation was gladly accepted. The date was September 8, 1886. The Archbishop ascended the pulpit to preach. For his text he took our Lord's words to Zacheus: "Today is salvation come to this house." The church was thronged to the limits of its capacity. In the midst of the sermon a curate from some neighboring parish arrived with a few young men. Through the open door they could see the preacher in the pulpit but they were unable to enter the church. Then the young priest said to them: "We cannot hear Archbishop Richard, but take a good look at him, remember his face; you can then say you have seen a saint."

The same thought had been expressed by Father Boin, the procurator at the Nantes seminary, who said, at the beginning of Bishop Richard's episcopacy: "In my life I have seen two saints, the Curé of Ars and Bishop Richard."

In the month of January, 1887, the Archbishop of Paris knelt at the feet of the Holy Father and asked the Pope's blessing upon his episcopacy. The next year he conducted to Rome a pilgrimage in honor of the sacerdotal jubilee of Leo XIII. Together with the Peter's pence, he presented to the Pope a superb tiara, the special gift of the clergy and faithful of Paris. From Rome the Archbishop wrote as follows:

With exquisite kindness, Leo XIII informed us as soon as we reached Rome that, in the solemnity of the jubilee

Mass, he wished to wear the tiara which was offered to him by the Capital of France. We were eager to go and, in your name, place it ourselves in his hands.

We should have liked to have you all there to assist at this solemnity, which rendered the first day of the year 1888 memorable in the feasts of the Church. Three hundred bishops surrounded the supreme pastor; with him, during the Mass, they recited the Nicene Creed, thus giving testimony to the faith of the Churches of the whole world. We have never experienced so profound an impression in the solemnities, which we have often witnessed, in this same Vatican Basilica.

On January 22, 1888, Archbishop Richard was called to Rome for the beatification of the Venerable Father de Montfort. The chapter of St. Peter's had especially invited him to celebrate the pontifical Mass and to intone the *Te Deum* in honor of the newly beatified servant of God, a native of Brittany. In June of the same year he was happy to take part in the triduum in honor of Blessed de Montfort, enthusiastically celebrated at St. Laurent-on-Sèvre in Vendée. Ever since Archbishop Richard had left Belley, he remained in correspondence with Mlle Ramisier, the devout promoter of the Eucharistic pilgrimages. These were changed into Eucharistic congresses, the sixth of which opened in Paris on July 2, 1888. The solemnities began at Notre Dame by the procession of the Blessed Sacrament and a sermon by

139

Father Monsabré. Four days later the Archbishop brought the congress to a close in the Montmartre basilica, where Bishop Mermillod spoke eloquently of our Lord's greatness and goodness in the Blessed Sacrament.

CHAPTER XII

Elevation to the Cardinalate

ARCHBISHOP RICHARD'S virtues attracted the attention of the Holy See. Spontaneously Leo XIII decided to make him a cardinal, although the French government was not at all inclined to beg any favors for him from the Pope. Archbishop Richard wrote to the Holy Father: "I have a feeling of confusion at seeing myself chosen for this lofty dignity in preference to so many other bishops whose virtues I venerate and whose talents I admire. But at the same time I feel deep gratitude for the goodness with which you have deigned to turn your eyes upon my humble person."

The chapter of the Nantes cathedral sent to the new Cardinal the pectoral cross of Bishop Affre, which had been worn also by Bishop Jaquemet. This precious relic was merely loaned to the Archbishop of Paris. The dean of the chapter wrote as follows: "When this cross, after being worn for many years to come, we hope, by the venerated Cardinal of Paris, is returned to the chapter treasury, of which it is now the principal gem, it will come back enriched with a new consecration that will enhance its value in the eyes of all."

The Belley chapter sent an address of felicitation to its former bishop. Congratulations arrived from all sides. With a delicacy characteristic of him, the new Cardinal decided to reply personally to each one, to the humblest as well as to the others. Thus he replied to the town council of Boussay:

"I have delayed replying to your felicitations because I wished to do so personally. I was greatly touched by the address which you sent to me on the occasion of my promotion to the cardinalate. I am always 'a boy of the Boussay parish,' as you remind me. With great pleasure I find at the end of your address the names of families that I esteem and that I have loved ever since the days of my youth. I will not cease asking the good God to keep the dear people of Boussay in the faith and the practice of the Christian virtues."

On Sunday, May 26, 1889, the Archbishop of Paris, created cardinal-priest of the Holy Roman Church, officially received the red zucchetto. At one o'clock in the afternoon His Eminence received

Prince Ruspoli, a noble guard of His Holiness Leo XIII, in the great drawing room, surrounded by Bishop Bélouino, the vicars general, the metropolitan chapter, and the members of the archiepiscopal family. A few days later, in the chapel of the archbishop's palace, took place the ceremony of the taking of the oath, in the presence of the papal nuncio, Bishop Rotelli, the ablegate Bishop Gasparri, assisted by Bishop Boudinhon and Prince Ruspoli.

Before the separation of the Church and state, the newly created cardinals went solemnly to the Elysée Palace for the imposition of the cardinalitial biretta. On the appointed day, the introducer of ambassadors came with four carriages from the President's palace to the Archiepiscopal palace, where the cardinals promoted at the last consistory, were gathered. They were: Cardinal Richard, Cardinal Foulon (archbishop of Lyons), and Cardinal Guilbert (archbishop of Bordeaux). The cardinals, the ablegates, and the noble guards with their suite, formed the cortege which was escorted by a squadron of cavalry.

At the President's palace all attended Mass in the chapel. At the close of the Mass the President, standing before the altar, placed the biretta on the Cardinal's head, and the introducer of ambassadors placed the red cloak on his shoulders. After this ceremony the cardinals were received by the President, and Cardinal Richard delivered the usual discourse.

The giving of the cardinal's hat took place at the consistory of December 30. Archbishop Richard, after ordinations on Ember Saturday, set out for Rome and reached there Christmas Eve.

While conforming to every prescription of the Roman ceremonial, the new Cardinal was especially mindful of the deep significance of the venerable ceremonies of the solemnity. Wholeheartedly he promised that loyalty to the Church, even to the shedding of his blood, which is symbolized by the cardinalitial red. That same day the title of Santa Maria in Via was assigned to him.

On January 14 he took possession of his titular church in the presence of a select but numerous gathering of people who attended. "Today," he said, "I bless God and thank Him for the portion of inheritance that He has given me in the Eternal City. . . . I am fond of invoking the Blessed Virgin under the title of Notre Dame of Paris. I shall now find joy in having at Rome the protection of the Blessed Virgin and in praying to her under the title of Santa Maria in Via."

The Cardinal returned to Paris, reaching there

at the end of January. The added reverence of clergy and faithful in no way lessened his simplicity and his close attachment to the people of his diocese. When giving them an account of the solemnities at Rome, he said: "We could not leave you strangers to what took place in our humble person, since we are happy to inform you of the marks of benevolence that the Holy Father has given to the Church of Paris, whose children you are."

A few months after his elevation to the cardinalate, Archbishop Richard was appointed by the Holy Father to preside over the ceremonies of the blessing and crowning of Our Lady of the Rosary at Lourdes. But, upon reaching Lourdes, he took to bed, suffering from illness which for a while caused serious anxiety. Thanks to the help of science and especially to the protection of the Immaculate Virgin, the ailment was checked. After a week's absence, he was back in Paris.

However, the doctors judged that a complete rest and especially the air of his native district were necessary to assure the full recovery of his imperiled health.

The news that the Cardinal was coming spread abroad at Boussay quickly. All vied with one another in their eagerness to give His Eminence a reception worthy of him. At about five o'clock in the evening a large throng of people had gathered at the entrance of the town to await his carriage. The street decorations gave evidence of the people's joy, and the good Cardinal entered the town amid loud cheers. Prompted by this joyous spirit, a venerable octogenarian presented a bouquet of flowers to him who was formerly called "Monsieur Francis." In the midst of a big procession of clergy and faithful eager to see him, Cardinal Richard passed along the streets toward the house of God. Promptly the church was filled with people. After an adoration of the Blessed Sacrament, mastering his fatigue, he expressed to those present his feelings upon coming for the first time as cardinal into the midst of a people that he always loved. The next Sunday he again addressed the people at the sermon time of the High Mass. In the evening at Vespers he gave the Benediction of the Blessed Sacrament. Several persons of the neighboring districts joined with the Boussay parishioners, gathered about the new prince of the Church.

During this time of convalescence, the good Cardinal used to visit the neighboring parishes. On September 11 he was received at Saint-Crespin by an enthusiastic crowd. A number of the Angers clergy had assembled to see him. Two priests from the diocese of Paris, natives of this district, had come to greet him. The Cardinal, speaking from the pulpit, said:

I am happy to be in the midst of you; I am not a stranger here; it is indeed now a long time since I came to this parish to greet Father Boisselier, the venerable predecessor of the present pastor. I no longer see here the church of my youth; many of those persons that I had seen are now gone. But I am happy to declare that the faith, far from being diminished here, seems to have grown. . . . The presence of one of my priests, Father Bouyer, recalls to my mind a pleasant memory, that of his venerable uncle, who was formerly a pastor in the city of Nantes and who gave me my first Communion.

After a short rest, the Cardinal prepared to depart. To gratify the people, he consented to go on foot as far as the entrance of the town. He advanced, continually smiling and blessing. The crowd of people pressed around him, the school children spread palms in his path. The people shouted: "Long live the Cardinal!" But he replied: "No my friends; but 'Long live Holy Church, long live Leo XIII!' "

At the end of this year the sixteenth centenary of the martyrdom of St. Donatian and St. Rogatian was celebrated. The zealous Father Hillereau, pastor of the parish of the Holy Martyrs, profited by the occasion to have the fine basilica consecrated.

It had just been completed. The good Cardinal, surrounded by several bishops, was pleased to preside at the festivities, which are an abiding memory in the minds of the people of Nantes.

Although all these ceremonies appealed to the heart of the Archbishop, they did not distract him from his regular labors. One of his ceaseless cares was to remain in closest union with the Holy See. Every year, in spite of the overwhelming burdens of his office, he made a rather prolonged stay at Rome to treat personally of the affairs of his diocese.

His attachment to the Supreme Pontiff and veneration for him appeared on every occasion. In the instructions issued by him he borrowed extensively from the encyclicals of Leo XIII. Sometimes these episcopal communications were really a commentary on the encyclicals, putting their contents and import within the grasp of the faithful. He liked to conduct French pilgrimages to the Eternal City. On March 2, 1893, he took part in the solemn audience of the cardinals and bishops present in Rome on the occasion of the Holy Father's jubilee and the double anniversary of his birth and his coronation. On December 27 of the next year Cardinal Richard's jubilee was celebrated at Paris. He had humbly thought to celebrate that fiftieth anniversary in silence and recollection; but the Paris clergy wished the date to be solemnly observed. At the religious ceremony in Notre Dame, Cardinal Perraud delivered a fine allocution; at the banquet in the Seminary of St. Sulpice, the Cardinal received, with his usual simplicity and humility, the expressions of felicitation expressed in several toasts. He did not for a moment forget the presence of God: he seemed to be examining his conscience about how he had made use of his fifty years of priesthood.

His priests had planned to offer him a gift as testimony of their filial regard. But the pious Archbishop, informed of this intention, immediately made known his wish that the money destined for the purchase of the remembrance should be employed for the erection of the high altar of Montmartre.

Outside of Paris the Cardinal's jubilee did not pass unnoticed. The Holy Father presented him with a gold medal, the diocese of Belley with a silver statue of the Curé of Ars; the Bishop of Nantes was represented at the jubilee festivities and celebrated, in the chapel of the Blessed Frances d'Amboise, a Mass at which a large assembly of the faithful was present. The people of Boussay gathered a fund among themselves so as to send him a miter ornamented with a medallion of St. Francis de Sales.

The jubilarian was deeply touched by these testimonies of respect and affection. To Cardinal Perraud he sent a gilded bronze reliquary containing a fragment of the true Cross and a bit of the crown of thorns, with this inscription: "To the most illustrious and most reverend Adolphe, Bishop of Autun, a brother who has given to his brother, on the fiftieth anniversary of his priesthood, the consolations and encouragement of his word full of faith and charity, Francis Richard, Archbishop of Paris, humbly returns thanks, December 27, 1894."

To the faithful, the good Cardinal distributed in large numbers images of Notre Dame of Paris, bearing this inscription on the reverse: "May the golden word of Blessed Frances d'Amboise be for all a blessing of our sacerdotal jubilee: Above all things else, strive that God may be better loved." Lastly, the charitable Archbishop could not, under these circumstances, forget the poor, whom he loved so much; and to the pastors of the poorest twenty parishes of Paris he sent alms for distribution.

CHAPTER XIII

The Cardinal's Labors

CARDINAL RICHARD'S incessant labors were interrupted only by prayer. His day began very early every morning. During the last years of his life, he consented to remain in bed somewhat longer: at first until four o'clock, then until half past four, then until a quarter to five, and at length until five o'clock.

As soon as he rose, he spent an hour in meditation, then he prepared for Mass, which he said at seven o'clock. After his thanksgiving and his breakfast, he devoted some time to the reading of Scripture and the recitation of the Little Hours. At a quarter before twelve, kneeling on a prie-dieu which in the former archiepiscopal residence was located between the two windows of his bedroom, he made his particular examination of conscience.

Whatever might be the circumstances, Cardinal Richard never neglected this practice of the par-

ticular examination. In October, 1896, the closing
of the fourteenth centenary of the baptism of Clovis
at Reims was festively celebrated. But the Cardinal was unable to leave his bedroom at noon to
go to the official dinner: his door latch had stuck,
and a locksmith had to be called. Of course the Cardinal was late in reaching the hall where cardinals,
archbishops, bishops, and other prelates were gathered. Cardinal Langénieux said to him: "Your
Eminence, you must have become impatient when
you found yourself locked in your own room."
"Not at all," he replied with a smile; "I took advantage of the opportunity to prolong my particular examen."

Every day the Archbishop read the Martyrology.
Before dinner he always recited the full form of
the table blessing, and at the close of the meal the
long form of thanksgiving. Then he went to the
chapel for a short adoration of the Blessed Sacrament before resuming his work. At about five
o'clock, after the day's interviews were concluded
and his correspondence attended to, he made
another visit to the Blessed Sacrament. In the
winter, at this hour he might be seen going down
the stairs, carrying his desk lamp, which he sometimes dropped on the stairs, to the great displeasure
of Joseph, his valet.

When traveling, the Cardinal adhered to his daily program so far as possible. This he could do the more easily since he had a compartment to himself on the train. He made his visit to the Blessed Sacrament, kneeling on the seat. This adoration he directed to the Blessed Sacrament in the churches whose spires he could see at a distance.

His piety was gentle, like that of St. Francis de Sales, his patron and model. His whole life was a continual prayer. In the presence of the divine Master he found the strength to perform his overwhelming labors. "Let us work, let us work," he often repeated to the priests of his household. The government of his immense diocese absorbed his time and strength, but he was devoted to his work with a zeal that some regarded as excessive. The long practice of the diocesan administration increased his experience but did not lessen his labor. Every good work, every organization, could count on his full devotedness and his active collaboration.

The title of Chancellor of the Catholic Institute was not regarded by the Cardinal as a merely honorary title. He was a practical support for the rector, Monsignor d'Hulst, and was at great pains to procure financial resources for the institution and to keep its teaching imbued with the purest doctrine. Monsignor d'Hulst's premature death was a grievous affliction for Cardinal Richard, but trials did not hinder his zeal. Three weeks later, at a solemn session of the Institute, recalling the memory of the lamented rector, he said: "Should we today merely stand still in the presence of regrets and memories? We have examples to gather together, generous resolutions to take." Monsignor Péchenard and later Monsignor Baudrillard, successively rectors of the Institute, always found in Cardinal Richard a true patron of their labors.

The Cardinal was exceedingly kind toward the various religious congregations, whose members he considered the elite of his flock. And they in turn considered him their particular bishop. He counted on their prayers to help him carry his heavy burden and to draw down the graces of heaven upon his vast diocese. Under his rule, religious communities increased in Paris. The diocesan council was sometimes concerned over the question of their increase and even feared that communities having the same end might perhaps work at cross-purposes. But the Cardinal said: "Paris is big, and the good to be done is immense: the workers will never be too many." Yet he was watchful that communities seeking admission into the diocese should not be able to harm those already established there. Like a military commander examining the plan of the citadel and marking the points that needed strengthening, he located on the map of Paris and its suburbs the districts already well cared for and, to communities asking admission, he pointed out the districts that were poorly provided where they could establish new works and where their presence would be a fruitful blessing.

Especially in times of trial Cardinal Richard showed his fatherly heart for the various congregations of his diocese.

In 1899, Waldeck-Rousseau, the prime minister, began his legal proceedings against religious houses. The first victims were the Assumptionists, who held a prominent place in the ranks of the French press. On January 24, 1900, a court decision imposed a fine on the members of the Association called the Congregation of the Augustinians of the Assumption, and declared the Association dissolved.

The next day the Cardinal went to their monastery to bring them a word of consolation in their trial. The government pretended to regard this action of the Archbishop as a political manifestation and requested the Vatican to reprimand him. The President of the Council wrote two haughty letters to the Cardinal, who replied to the first with a firm dignity, and sent a copy of his reply to Leo XIII.

On January 29, the feast day of St. Francis de Sales, his patron, the Cardinal received from Rome, at about eight o'clock in the evening, from his suffragan, the Bishop of Orleans, then present in Rome, a rather obscure telegram announcing that an explanatory letter would follow. This letter arrived on the 31st. Bishop Touchet, with becoming deference, related to him what had taken place. Cardinal Rampolla had called him to the Vatican and asked him to send a telegram to Cardinal Richard: "His purpose was to put an end to any manifestations following upon the affair of the Assumptionists, any manifestations by the clergy or by friends of the Assumption."

On Thursday, February 1, at four o'clock in the afternoon, the Nuncio came to see the Cardinal, whom he found confined to bed by an attack of grippe. The interview lasted half an hour. Upon leaving the Cardinal's bedroom, the Nuncio looked annoyed. The Cardinal's private secretary accompanied him to the foot of the great stairs. In the vestibule, the Nuncio spoke only this one sentence: "Something has to be surrendered to the flames in order to save the rest of the building." As to the

Cardinal, the high color of his cheeks and an increase of fever indicated that the explanation with the Nuncio had not been altogether tranquil.

The Cardinal remained silent about what took place at that interview. But in the papers which he has left on this affair, there is one document by which we can easily surmise it. The Nuncio had come to communicate the contents of a note sent by Cardinal Rampolla, in which, while paying respects to the Archbishop's intentions, the papal Secretary of State directed that an end be put to manifestations that might be interpreted in a political sense and might produce an effect the very opposite of that hoped for.

About a week later the Cardinal received a letter in Leo XIII's own hand, replying to his letter of January 28. The Pope praised his zeal and his spirit of charity. However, he added that, if he had been consulted, he would have given counsel that perhaps would have prevented the recent events. The government had asked that the Archbishop be censured. The Pope sent his advice, preceded by words of praise. The Cardinal received it with admirable humility, saying: "When Rome knows the truth, it will certainly approve what I have done." In fact, that is what happened.

Cardinal Richard showed a warm devotion for

all the Paris shrines, among which the Notre Dame Cathedral held first place. To his clergy he wrote: "Our ancient metropolitan church of Notre Dame stirs our religious affection because it bears the title of the Blessed Virgin, who does not disdain being invoked there under the name of Notre Dame of Paris."

On November 10, 1793, the Revolution hatefully installed in Notre Dame the worship of the goddess Reason. On November 12, 1893, the Cardinal celebrated a ceremony of reparation in the church that had been profaned a hundred years earlier. He read an act of reparation that revealed the fervor of his soul. The attendance was so large that a throng of people who could not gain admittance stood outside in the square.

The relics in the possession of Notre Dame treasury were an object of particular veneration for the devout Archbishop. For the holy crown of thorns of our Lord, he had a reliquary made of rock crystal, ornamented with a lattice-work in pure gold, and enriched with diamonds and various gems.

The Cardinal was fond of praying at Notre Dame des Victoires, at the Foreign Mission Seminary on rue du Bac, and in the chapel of the miraculous medal, where he derived strength and comfort.

He also liked particularly the Montmartre basilica of the Sacred Heart. He had come to Paris immediately after the laying of the cornerstone of this church; for thirty-two years he gave to the Committee the aid of his devotedness, his competence, and his wisdom. On June 17, 1689, St. Margaret Mary had asked, in the name of our Lord, the reign of the Sacred Heart over France. Two centuries later, on June 28, 1889, on the feast of the Sacred Heart, there took place in the Montmartre basilica the first consecration of France to the Sacred Heart by Cardinal Richard. Most of the bishops of France were assembled at that consecration, which thus assumed a national character.

On June 5, 1891, Cardinal Richard blessed the church, assisted by two other cardinals and eighteen bishops. Four years later he blessed the bell, called the Savoyarde, whose sonorous voice would, like the great bell of Notre Dame, dominate the noise of Paris. After another four years, when Leo XIII consecrated the whole human race to the Sacred Heart, the Cardinal, then eighty years old, climbed to the top of the great dome and placed there the

159

cross that overlooks the Capital. The next year, on the first feast of the Sacred Heart in the twentieth century, he solemnly inaugurated this dome and the four cupolas that surround it. On June 16, 1905, he laid the cornerstone of the campanile intended to house the Savoyarde.

Every year, on the feast of the Sacred Heart, he came to Montmartre and there celebrated low Mass at nine o'clock. At the Gospel of the Mass he preached briefly from the pulpit. In spite of his advanced age, he continued to give Communion to large numbers of the faithful. It would have been a disappointment for them not to receive Communion from the hand of the saint, as they called him. When eventually he had to allow a priest to assist him, the people obstinately waited on the side where His Eminence was distributing Communion. Then the priest would have to withdraw and leave the Cardinal alone to give Communion to the waiting throng.

After a light breakfast, he went to the convent of the Religious of the Cenacle, a community that had been recently established on Montmartre. With fatherly kindness he took an interest in the community and its works. Before leaving he spoke a few words that inflamed their hearts with love for the divine heart of Jesus. At noon he gathered at a friendly dinner the Committee of the National Vow, the chaplains of the basilica, and the members of his episcopal family. After dinner he visited in detail the various parts of the basilica under construction. Up to his last years he might be seen, followed by the Committee, climbing the high scaffoldings and having the architect give him a minute report about the progress of the work. At three o'clock he presided at solemn Vespers in the basilica and was present at the sermon. At the close of the Benediction the Cardinal departed without showing the least sign of weakness, although the ceremony had lasted three hours. He often remarked: "Instead of feeling fatigue, I seem to have regained my strength."

Whenever the Cardinal had a particularly serious preoccupation, he sent word that he would say his Mass on such and such a day at the Montmartre basilica. "How many graces," he said, "the Sacred Heart grants there!" As he prayed there for France, often he repeated: "Here is to be found the salvation of our poor country. What would become of Paris if it did not have Notre Dame des Victoires and Montmartre?"

The basilica of St. Denis, patron of the diocese, was threatened by the public authorities; a socialist city government wished to turn it into a court house. But the Cardinal succeeded in having it made a parish church. His special devotion to St. Genevieve, also a patron saint of Paris, prompted him to have her statue placed in his cardinalitial church of Santa Maria in Via in Rome.

In a populous quarter of Paris, on the slope of Belleville, a large, beautiful church, in Roman style, had been built during the Second Empire and dedicated to St. Joseph. The Cardinal decided to have it solemnly consecrated and to profit by the occasion to consecrate the city and the diocese to the head of the holy family.

As the population of Paris increased year by year, the existing churches were insufficient for public worship. With tireless perseverance Cardinal Richard had new churches built. Government financial assistance was lacking. But in response to his appeal Christian charity responded with admirable faith and thus several new churches were erected.

The Cardinal was familiar with all the parishes of his vast diocese. He made a close study of the administration and activities of each one. Whenever he appointed a new pastor to one of these, he explained the conditions of the parish to him with such exactness that a certain Paris priest once said: "I have been in this parish for ten years; but I am not now better acquainted with it than I was on the day His Eminence appointed me to it."

Religious ignorance and indifference grieved the Cardinal. To remedy conditions and to increase the number of sermons and missions, he founded a group of diocesan missioners and encouraged their zeal wholeheartedly.

During Lent of 1893 the diocesan missioners gave a series of conferences on the great Christian virtues in the Church of St. Denis. The freethinkers of the city planned to attend and to interrupt the preacher. On March 26, without any provocation on the part of the preacher, a member of the city council, standing up in front of the pulpit, insisted on speaking. Father Lenfant, who was in the pulpit, suggested to him that he put his objection in writing. This peaceful proposal was displeasing to the friends of the brazen councilor. In the ensuing fight ten persons were wounded.

Father Lenfant relates: "On March 27 I went to see His Eminence and laid the facts before him. Then I asked him: 'Your Eminence, can you come tomorrow?' 'Why not?' I told him with a smile that a report was in circulation to the effect that the mayor of St. Denis had said: 'If the Archbishop comes, he will be carried back in pieces.' "

The Cardinal, not hesitating for a moment, an-

163

swered: "But what is said by those whose business it is to assure good order?"

"They say that you may come if you so desire."

"Very well, I will go."

That same evening Father Iteney announced to his agitated parishioners, prepared to defend their pastor: "This will be your reward; tomorrow the Cardinal will come." The next day the Archbishop arrived in his modest carriage, escorted by a few mounted gendarmes, whom he had certainly not asked for. About twenty gendarmes, revolver in hand, were in the church, two of them at the foot of the pulpit. At the close of the sermon, His Eminence rose and, in a gentle voice, said: "I have come more than once into this church, but never with so great joy or in the midst of so large a number of the faithful." Then he thanked those present, spoke of the strength to be found in the Christian faith, said a few words about the Church and the Supreme Pontiff, and returned, calm and smiling, through the animated throng, to his carriage. He was as undisturbed as if he were in the parlor of the episcopal residence.

The suppression of religious instruction in the schools placed on the Cardinal a stricter obligation to consider the teaching of catechism to the children. He urged special attention to this duty

164

and encouraged the work of the volunteer catechists. "To restore the knowledge of God and of our Lord to its position of honor in families," he established religious examinations and distributions of prizes, at which he himself presided at Notre Dame.

Cardinal Richard's solicitude extended to all the Catholic schools of Paris. As formerly at Nantes and at Belley, he was fond of visiting the many educational establishments of Paris, to bring to the teachers and pupils his fatherly encouragement. So, when Combes, the prime minister, turned his attacks against Catholic schools, the Cardinal promptly wrote to the President of the Republic an indignant protest against the injustice of the sectarian laws. In this letter he said:

The measures that have been taken manifest the evident intention to close the schools, after everything has been combined to attain that end. . . . But, with the help of God, we will continue to perform our duty as a bishop and a French bishop. We will defend the liberty of Christian families in the education of their children, we will defend the liberties that are our rights as citizens. . . . We do not ask for privileges, but we demand that the Catholics shall not be deprived of the rights that belong to all French citizens. . . . The voice of those who are suffering may not reach you, Mr. President; perhaps ours will be heard.

If we are no longer astonished at the undeserved rigors

imposed on us, yet not without deep sorrow have we seen presented to the Chamber of Deputies, in the name of the President of the Republic, a project which has for its purpose not simply to destroy at one blow all the teaching religious congregations, but besides, Christian teaching itself.

A strict account must be rendered to God and to posterity by those who have charge of the education of the people. They will have to answer for these millions of children brought up without faith, without morals, without respect, and they will know that, in the scales of divine justice, the tears poured out in Christian homes and in all our religious communities weigh heavily.

Completely ignoring the protests of the Catholics, the government rigorously applied the education laws. The Cardinal gave encouragement and example for all sacrifices to safeguard the souls of the children at any cost.

The eternal salvation of the sick, deprived of priests and of sisters in the laicized hospitals, was also a matter of ceaseless concern to the Archbishop. In 1896 he wrote as follows: "Ever since the chaplains were removed from our hospitals I have been in the habit of reciting daily, three times a day for the dying, the prayer, 'Most merciful Jesus, have pity on the dying.' " So far as lay in his power he continued to sustain the hospital work.

The disturbed times aroused new devices of zeal. Cardinal Richard extended his favor both to the works already established and to those which the new circumstances brought forth: the Society of St. Vincent de Paul, other pious and apostolic works, nocturnal adoration, professional associations, works of charity, youth movements, patronages, circles, and so forth. At the diocesan headquarters he centralized the direction of the activities of the diocese. None of them was a stranger to him, and he was watchful that they should remain in full conformity with pure doctrine. For the foundation of these works and their fruitful apostolate Providence assured him, among the priests and the laity, of helpers with an inexhaustible devotedness. Such were Father Roussel, founder of the Auteuil orphanage; Monsignor Rozier, director of the work of adoption; Vicomte de Melun, founder of the Paris patronages; M. Beluze, founder of the students' circles; M. Chesnelong and M. Keller, successive presidents of the Society of Education and Instruction. Madame de Melun and Madame de Ladoucette founded the organization for working girls. Marshal MacMahon for a long time was at the head of the work of Mercy; in the little chapel of Bishop de Segur was born the Catholic association of French youth with Count Albert de Mun as sponsor.

The Cardinal was at first favorable to the Catholic and social movement of the *Sillon,* but soon its tendencies gave him cause for anxiety. He offered fatherly advice, then he admonished it. In 1907 the *Sillon* took a definite turn, as a purely political and social work, thus becoming independent and withdrawn from the direct control of the bishops. Thereafter the Cardinal maintained a reserved attitude toward it.

His apostolic zeal was not limited to his diocese, not even to France. The purpose of his life was to extend the kingdom of God everywhere. Time and again he recommended to the prayers of the faithful the conversion of Protestant England; with this intention he established a monthly Mass at Notre Dame des Victoires. The Catholics of the Orient and all the foreign missions had a place in his prayers and in his exhortations to the people of his diocese.

The Cardinal followed with close attention the work of the missioners, not only by his reading of the *Annals of the Propagation of the Faith* and of *Catholic Missions,* but also by his personal correspondence with a large number of missioners. Father Babonneau, a Marist, native of Boussay, used to speak of the encouragement he received from Cardinal Richard during the latter's visits to Boussay. When Father Babonneau became a missioner in the Solomon Islands he used to write to the Cardinal, telling about his far-off apostolic labors.

As formerly at Nantes and at Belley, Cardinal Richard was happy to pay homage to the saints. He was greatly pleased at the beatification of Father de Montfort, John Baptist de la Salle, Father John Gabriel Perboyre, the martyrs of China, and Father Clet. He recommended to the prayers of the faithful the new causes, wishing particularly to see placed on the altars Joan of Arc, Father Olier, Louise de Marillac, the martyrs of the Revolution, the Carmelites of Compiègne, Madame Louise of France, Madame de Bonnault d'Houët, Sister Catherine Labouré, Venerable Mother de Sales Chappuis, Father Eymard, Venerable Mother Barat, and the martyrs of the Commune.

The closest union existed between Cardinal Richard and his clergy. He encouraged the zeal of the young priests, and surrounded with esteem the veterans of the priesthood. To all he showed his interest, and shared the joys as well as the sufferings of each one.

He had a fatherly heart for his priests, a charity that extended to all, even to priests that did not belong to the diocese. He received them and corresponded with them. For him this was a sort of special apostolate that he cherished very much.

169

His solicitude reached out even to those who had strayed, whom he tried to recall to the right way. He prayed continually for the unfortunate Father Hyacinth and every year received a report about him from Father Franck, a most worthy priest, who owed his conversion to the apostate. While yet a child, the little Franck, who was a Protestant, innocently turned for instruction in catechism to the chapel which had been opened by the former Father Hyacinth. When the poor fallen-away saw with whom he was dealing, he said to the boy: "I am not the one you should go to. Rather go see your pastor." And that is what the young Franck did. But Father Hyacinth always kept a friendly interest in his caller. Father Franck profited by this attitude to make an annual visit to the former religious.

The Archbishop of Paris exercised an active vigilance to preserve his clergy and his faithful from errors against the faith. At Paris more than elsewhere the books, periodicals, newspapers, lectures, public debates, the conversation at social gatherings, rapidly sowed harmful doctrines. The dangerous tendencies that have been comprised under the name of modernism were matters of serious concern to Cardinal Richard. His clear vision and firmness had removed from the Catholic

Institute the teaching of Loisy, without, however, preserving Loisy himself from the paths of error.

However absorbed in the spiritual government of his diocese, Cardinal Richard was not a stranger to any contemporary event. His charitable compassion made him share in the public mourning. He presided at Marshal MacMahon's obsequies at the Invalides, and went himself to the bedside of the dying Marshal Canrobert; he assisted General Dessirier, governor of Paris, at his last moments. When a catastrophe, such as the burning of the Opera Comique in 1887 or that of the Metropolitain in 1903, afflicted the city, the Cardinal wrote letters full of Christian consolation for the desolated families.

On May 4, 1897, he was at Rome at the time of the terrible fire of the Charité bazar. Hastily he returned to Paris telegraphing the Holy Father's blessing to the bereaved families. On May 8 he presided at Notre Dame at the religious services held for the victims, among whom was a princess of the House of France, the Duchess d'Alençon. The Cardinal went in person with his condolences to the Duke d'Alençon, to the president of the Charité bazar, the Baron de Mackau, the Roland-Gosselin family, the superior of the Daughters of Charity. A year later, on the site of the catastrophe, the Cardinal blessed the cornerstone of a commemorative chapel and gave it the name of Our Lady of Consolation.

In fact, the Cardinal took a part in all important contemporary events by the simple performance of the duty of public prayer, which his conscience directed him to fulfill and which his patriotism led him to recall to the representatives of the country. Over and over, despite appearances to the contrary, he used to repeat: "The soul of France is Christian." Hence he experienced great pleasure when a large number of Catholics in 1890 requested him to order prayers for France at the opening of the Chambers. Each year he renewed this ceremony at Notre Dame, and also every year, at the time of the opening of the courts, he presided at the solemn Mass of the Holy Ghost, called the Red Mass on account of the color of the vestments.

The Madagascar expedition and that to China called forth his zeal. He invoked God's blessing on the French armies and celebrated their success by the singing of the *Te Deum* at Notre Dame. The lay laws suppressed the military chaplains. But Cardinal Richard, always solicitous for the welfare of souls, at once placed at the disposal of the Minister of War some volunteer chaplains. The spiritual welfare of the army was always a matter of concern to the Cardinal, who had numerous military Masses, retreats, and circles at Paris, to which he frequently went in person.

Not wishing the Universal Exposition of 1900, which attracted visitors from all nations, to be devoid of every religious idea, he appointed a committee to promote the participation of Catholic works at the Exposition. He said: "This will be an act of the apostolate calculated to show, in some little way, the benefits which society has received and still receives from the Christian religion."

There being no official religious organization in connection with the Exposition, the Cardinal presided at a solemn Mass at Notre Dame. To this Mass he invited all those participating in the Exposition; the cathedral was filled. A magnificent sermon by Father Coubé gave great lustre to this imposing ceremony. At the request of the Swiss and Belgians who were attached to the Exposition, he organized a religious service for persons connected with it, in the parishes near the Palace of the Champ-de-Mars.

In his dealings with the government, the Cardinal's attitude was one of reserve. With the chief government officials he was dignified and courteous, but he always performed his duty by speaking the truth. He appeared simple and unrestrained at the loftiness of his office and, when circumstances required, he faced the public authorities as a prince of the Church and as Archbishop of Paris. The hypocritical and brutal religious persecution which showed itself in the decree about the fabriques and in the law about the congregations, was opposed by the Cardinal with passive resistance. This attitude accorded with his character, which was resistant rather than combative, but resistant to the end with the tenacity of a Breton. He himself said: "It will not be said that the bishops accepted all these injustices without protest. We must resist; this we owe to ourselves, to the Church of France, and to history which will some day say that we have done our duty." "But," someone remarked, "finally it will always be necessary to pay." "Possibly," he replied, "it is even certain, but we must yield only under constraint and force, we must not accept the injustice of our own accord. We must not go at the first summons and be in haste to turn over to the state our accounts and our funds. First we should exhaust every means of delay: the gaining of time is much, because time belongs to God."

Whenever he received from the government office of the Director of Worship those letters which, in language intentionally discourteous, informed him of some fresh attacks upon the liberty of the

Church, the Cardinal, when conveying the news to his council, added merely: "I am putting this letter aside; I will take my time in answering it." When the situation grew worse, he declared to those about him: "I have waited, I have reflected, I have prayed, I cannot keep silent any longer, my duty is to speak; I am going to write to the President of the Republic." He had no illusions about the effect of his letters. But he regarded them not merely as writings; they were acts. Under these circumstances he felt that silence might be looked upon as complicity. He must free his own conscience and, as head of the episcopate, speak to the head of the state in the firm and restrained language of justice.

In 1886, when Bishop Richard became archbishop of Paris, M. Dumay was appointed Director of Public Worship. For twenty years he had more or less direct dealings with the Cardinal and eagerly seized every occasion to be disagreeable to him. He watched and waited for the Cardinal's death, that he might designate one of his own creatures to the see of Paris. In December, 1904, the Cardinal was seriously ill, and Edgard Combes, secretary to the Minister of the Interior, telephoned to the Director of Public Worship that the Archbishop was dying. At once M. Dumay sent the deputy justice of peace to put the seals on the house of the deceased Cardinal. The move was a little premature: M. Dumay died three years before Cardinal Richard. During the Cardinal's long pontificate, every year, notwithstanding the Holy Father's attempts to solicit tolerance, the government's religious hostility became more and more accentuated.

Without regard for consciences and without concern for the past, they set to work to laicize all France, in its schools, its hospitals, all the national institutions. In a pastoral letter dated September 29, 1887, the Archbishop of Paris spoke to the people of his diocese about this peril, saying:

> The secularization is being carried on by institutions under cover of a word with uncertain and doubtful meaning, "laicization." They laicize the laws, they laicize all the acts of law from birth to the tomb; they laicize the family by laws destructive of the Christian doctrine of marriage; they laicize teaching by the so-called neutrality of the school; they laicize the works and establishments of charity by removing whatever can bear the mark of a religious thought.

Wicked laws followed one after the other. The law of the fabriques, laws against the religious, laws against the teaching congregations, expulsions and spoliation of the communities, and so on.

All these laws were harshly applied under

176

Waldeck-Rousseau and Combes, in spite of the Cardinal's indignant protests.

On April 17, 1903, he wrote to M. Combes:

On the point perhaps of appearing before God to give an account of my burdensome office, I am not conscious of having ever disturbed the public order in the dioceses that have been entrusted to me; nor am I conscious of having ever failed in my duty as pastor of souls, by neglecting to protest against measures tending to the oppression of consciences and to the destruction of religion in our beloved country.

In 1904 came the rupture with the Vatican. The next year the separation of Church and state was voted. Article 2 of the separation law contained this expression: "The Republic recognizes no public worship." These words, more than any others, affected the Cardinal painfully. "What they wish," he repeated, "is to laicize the Church. It is the destruction of religion, it is the plan pursued by the antichristian sects."

Soon began the inventory of the churches, new vexations and spoliations, before the time came to expel the Cardinal himself from his own archiepiscopal residence. Cardinal Richard with an experienced eye observed these painful events and maintained a firm dignity. His humility had always kept him from seeking the first place, but at that period he appeared as the true head of the Church of France.

Although on every occasion Cardinal Richard showed himself the intrepid defender of the rights of the Church, his unshakable firmness did not keep him from exercising his boundless charity, even toward the persons who had most offended him. In the individuals he always saw the souls that he strove to save by bringing them to God.

In the month of October, 1899, a strike of the laborers broke out in the nearby Exposition. Things took a disquieting turn, and several regiments of cavalry were sent to Paris to maintain order. There was reason to fear a conflict between the workmen and the soldiers. Certain important persons urged the Cardinal to intervene. He did not at once reject this idea, but, according to his habit, made a personal inquiry about the causes of the strike. "After duly reflecting, consulting, and praying," he said at length, "I am convinced that this strike is not social, but political. I have therefore no cause to interfere. If they take a bad turn and if bloody strife takes place in the streets, then I will do as Bishop Affre did, I will go."

While speaking thus, forcefully but with complete simplicity, the Cardinal held his pectoral cross in his right hand, the very cross worn by Bishop Affre when he fell a martyr of his charity, the cross which came from Bishop Jaquemet. The Cardinal stood erect in an energetic attitude. That same evening, in his study, lighted by a little lamp, Cardinal Richard appeared truly great.

Cardinal Richard shared the joys as well as the griefs of France. The Russian alliance did not leave him indifferent. In October, 1893, he received at his house Admiral Avellane and the officers of the Russian navy. He had the *Te Deum* sung in the Montmartre basilica. Three years later he paid a visit to Czar Nicholas II at the Russian embassy. Surrounded by his vicars general and his chapter, he received the Czar at Notre Dame and had the *Te Deum* sung. He was also present at the dinner given at the Elysée to the Russian sovereigns. In 1891, at the suggestion of M. de Laboulaye, the French ambassador to St. Petersburg, he offered to Alexander III the holy banners that had been taken at Sebastopol and placed in Notre Dame. Czar Nicholas retained so pleasant a memory of his relations with the Archbishop of Paris that, several years later, when the Assumptionists sought permission to establish themselves at St. Petersburg, Vilna, and Odessa, the Czar replied that they must have their request backed by Cardinal Richard, for whom he had a profound esteem and to whom he could not refuse anything.

On May 31, 1905, the Cardinal was happy to receive at Notre Dame, with the ceremonial reserved for Catholic rulers, the young King of Spain, Alfonso XIII. At the door of the basilica he presented the holy water to the sovereign and addressed him with these words:

> Sire, it is an honor and a pleasure for me to offer to Your Majesty the homage of the clergy and people of this great Capital of France. To this homage we add sincere prayers for the prosperity of your reign which begins under happy auspices. We are pleased to pray with you, Sire, in this ancient cathedral, which keeps the religious and patriotic souvenirs of our France. You are not a stranger here. At Notre Dame your ancestors prayed to our St. Louis, whose name is venerated throughout the world. Here it was that Louis XIII made the vow, the memory of which we celebrate each year, to consecrate France to the Blessed Virgin. Today, Sire, we offer the same prayer for Spain and for France. We will gratefully remember Her Majesty the Queen, your mother. All admire her and thank her for giving to Catholic Spain a king so worthy of it.

The King modestly replied: "Such I am not yet, but with the grace of God, I will strive to become so."

As they mounted the steps of the sanctuary, the young King assisted the aged Archbishop. A few hours later, a criminal attack was made upon the

King of Spain, and the Cardinal was deeply moved by it.

In private life as in official ceremonies, Cardinal Richard showed unfailingly an equable disposition that was one of the charms of his character. When receiving callers, he was amiable, attentive, patient, never appearing to be in a hurry. So completely did he give his attention and interest to the person speaking to him, that he seemed not to have any other business, however many visitors might be waiting to see him. Simple and distinguished in manner, he always carried himself suitably, whether he was receiving the Queen of Spain and the princes of the House of France in the reception room adjoining his study or whether, in the salon on the ground floor, adjoining the chapel, he was receiving the members of a traveling circus whom he had just confirmed.

His kindheartedness led him to be ceaselessly concerned with the poor and the lowly, whom he was particularly fond of. Every year on March 19, the feast of the Patronage of St. Joseph, he went to one of the houses of the Little Sisters of the Poor. He would put on a white apron and serve the old men; then he received their thanks in one of the refectories turned into a reception hall. To the old man who voiced their thanks to him, he replied with the greatest kindness, and invariably began with these words: "I too am one of you, because I am old, even older than many of you."

In 1904 he presided at the funeral of Bishop Goux in the Versailles Cathedral. When the time came for him to give the absolution, before taking the cope he prepared to put on the amice over his rochet: the amice was not at hand. The master of ceremonies was thus much upset. "It is always like that on big ceremonies," the Cardinal said smiling. To the master of ceremonies, who spoke to the sacristan a bit sharply, the Cardinal then said: "Be sure that you do not scold him."

One day a Sister of St. Vincent de Paul attached to the Italian work, while speaking to the Cardinal, said to him that, during Monsignor Gasparri's vacation, she had much trouble in finding a priest who spoke Italian to assist a dying Italian workman. Then the Cardinal suggested to her that the next time if she would come after him he himself would go to assist the dying man.

Cardinal Richard took particular interest in the ragmen of Paris, who formed a population apart. One day, giving first Communion to a number of these poor people, he wished, as in the days when he was coadjutor, to go himself to the house of a dying young man who had not received confirma-

182

tion. To reach the attic the Archbishop had to climb a ladder. On his knees in this wretched hovel, the good Cardinal spoke words of comfort to the dying man and recited aloud the prayers in his place. All who were present were moved to tears. Before the door of the house the ragpickers were closely crowded to surround their archbishop at his leaving.

Every day requests for help piled up on the Archbishop's desk. Some of the poor addressed letters to him without putting any postage stamp on the envelope, calling him on the envelope, "His Majesty the Cardinal." The postoffice, seeing from the writing and the spelling that the sender was a client of the Cardinal, did not charge postage due on the letter. This was a delicate manner of associating themselves with the Archbishop's charity. From time to time he received requests from people of Nantes, who had the name "Richard" and claimed relationship with him. The good Cardinal smilingly said: "I think I would not blush to have poor relatives; but I search my memory in vain to find any relatives by the name of Richard; there are none any more at Nantes."

Apart from his short vacations and some journeys for religious ceremonies or family reasons, the Cardinal rarely left his diocese.

In 1890 he went to Belley for the festivities of the beatification of Blessed Pierre Chanel. During the journey he read over the sermon that he was to preach. As sometimes happened to him, he fell asleep. Of a sudden he woke up and said to his secretary: "You have just seen something that you will not often see in the course of your life: a preacher sleeping during his own sermon."

The annual journey to Rome was his only distraction. There he found souvenirs of his priestly youth. It was not, however, a rest for him; he gave all his time to business matters. Cardinal Gotti said: "Cardinal Richard arouses our admiration. He goes to the Congregations with his documents and personally handles all his affairs."

At Rome, as at Paris and elsewhere, the poor knew his inexhaustible charity. A line of beggars, learning of his arrival from the newspapers, was waiting for him at the door of the Procure of St. Sulpice. And there they were whenever his carriage went in or out. They used to say to one another: "The Cardinal of Paris is very rich." His secretary tried to keep these persistent beggars at a distance. But the Cardinal would not let him do so. One day he saw an aged couple there, and handed them a little sum of money. "These poor people," he said, "will now have a little feast; they will drink a *picolo* to my health and will pray for me."

At the time of one of these annual visits to Rome, even before the Cardinal's arrival there came to the Procure seventy letters all from the same street, in the neighborhood of St. Mary Major's. They were requests for help, all in the same hand, that of the public writer. The procurator thought he ought simply destroy them. When the Cardinal was told of the incident, he did what our Lord did when the disciples were keeping the importunate crowd of mothers from coming to Him.

In 1903, upon the death of Leo XIII, the Cardinal, then eighty-four years old, at once set out for Rome in spite of the oppressive heat. On July 31 he left the Procure of St. Sulpice and went to the Vatican, there to occupy the modest apartment reserved for him. His edifying piety prompted Cardinal Vives to say later: "He is the Curé of Ars of the Sacred College."

On the morning of August 4, after the last balloting, the voice of Cardinal Richard, the dean of the tellers of the conclave, called out fifty times the name of Cardinal Joseph Sarto. The election of the Pope was completed.

Cardinal Richard had but slight acquaintance with the new Pope. When Pius X had been vested with the papal robes, each of the cardinals in turn knelt before him for the first homage, which was soon followed by the solemn homage.

That evening the Archbishop of Paris left the Vatican. The members of his party were concerned for his health, but his moral vigor kept up his strength to the end. On the evening of August 4 he was filled with supernatural joy and thanksgiving, and the following morning took part in the solemn audience in the Sistine Chapel. But the succession of ceremonies and visits, the emotional strain of the conclave, however consoling its conclusion, had added to his fatigue. He was unable to be present at the coronation of Pius X five days later.

The doctor advised his immediate departure for Paris, with a night's rest at Bourg. The climate of France conquered his fatigue and dispelled all anxiety for his health. On the evening of his arrival at Paris he made an address to his servants gathered in his private chapel for night prayers; he spoke to them about the Holy Father and the loyalty which all Christians owe to the Vicar of Christ. Two days later he went to Notre Dame to celebrate the feast of the Assumption.

Soon Pius X's first encyclical appeared. The Cardinal was much impressed by it and repeated again and again the Holy Father's motto: "To restore all things in Christ."

Two months and a half after the conclave, Cardinal Richard returned to Rome that he might express his filial devotion *viva voce*. This he did in the long audiences which the Supreme Pontiff granted him.

On every visit to Rome the Cardinal habitually made a pilgrimage to the great basilicas—St. Peter's, St. Paul's outside the walls, and St. John Lateran's, the mother of churches. He also went to the Scala Santa, and mounted these steps on his knees, slowly because of his age. It might, indeed, well be considered the first of the stations of the Cross.

He invariably made it a duty to call upon all the cardinals then in Rome and upon all the French religious communities. This burdensome program, which he imposed on himself at every visit to the Eternal City, was likewise carried out during his stay there in October, 1903. Without realizing the fact, that time he was making his farewell visits. His declining strength did not permit him to undertake so long a journey again.

CHAPTER XIV

The Cardinal's Vacations

AMID his numerous labors, the Cardinal took a short vacation every year, usually dividing his time among his relatives at Nantes, l'Echasserie, and la Vergne.

At Nantes he stayed at the house of the Missioners of the Immaculate Conception. As soon as his arrival became known, rich and poor flocked to the little parlor, where the good prelate received them with his customary affability. Then he began his visits, starting with his niece, Mlle Léonide Pellerin de la Vergne, whose age was almost the same as his own and whom he called "the matriarch of the family."

Besides these visits to his nephews and nieces, he continued his relations of earlier years. So far as his absorbing duties allowed, especially in celebrating their weddings, he liked to pay homage to "those noble families, those Christians of an old and noble race." He radiated the charm of his amiability in the homes that he visited, and he forgot no one. General Fririon, upon learning that the Cardinal was at Carquefou, at the home of one of his nephews, wished to go at once to present his respects; but, out of consideration of the general's advanced age, the Cardinal himself set out to pay him a call. On the way he met the old army officer and said to him: "General, I am going to make you retreat; this will be the first time you ever did so."

After the stay at Nantes, the Cardinal divided his time between l'Echasserie and la Vergne. On the way, as he passed through Clisson he always left his carriage and knelt at the grave of Father Lefort, formerly secretary of the Bishop of Nantes.

The word of his coming spread rapidly at Boussay. The streets were decorated, bonfires were prepared, the clergy, accompanied by the school children, set out to meet him. As soon as the carriage came in sight, the whole population pressed forward to greet him with joyous shouts. His face brightened with a happy smile when he stepped out of his carriage into the midst of his friends. First he greeted the pastor; then he traced a cross on the foreheads of his kneeling grandnephews and great-grandnephews; lastly some of the children handed him some matches, and the bonfires were soon

189

crackling, while the church bells rang out with all their might. The carriage went off without him, and the Cardinal crossed the town on foot. Men, women, the old folks and the little children, knelt along his route. "May God bless you, my good friends," he repeated, "I am happy to be among you." The crowd accompanied him in procession to the church, where, after an adoration of the Blessed Sacrament, he recited aloud an Our Father and a Hail Mary. Then, standing before the altar, he addressed a few words to the people, expressing his joy at being again in this dear parish, to which he still belonged at heart, among families that he so loved and among whom he hoped to find always the same traditions of religious faith and practice. During his last years the people had to strain their ears to hear him, but the words "faith," "keep the faith," they could hear repeated again and again.

After leaving the church, the Cardinal went to la Vergne, where the servants, the farm tenants, and the people of the neighboring villages were waiting for his special blessing. One of them, deeply moved by the atmosphere of holiness which enveloped the Archbishop, cried out: "When Monsignor is here, it is almost as if the good God were here."

The family circle especially rejoiced at receiving

its venerated head. Everything was done to make him feel the welcome of this home of his childhood: the mistress of the house reserved to herself the privilege of filling her uncle's holy-water vessel at the last moment. Once or twice, busy with her many preparations, she had forgotten to do so. But as soon as the Cardinal entered, his valet asked for the holy water. In his own home, as also in the archiepiscopal residence, Cardinal Richard never entered his room without making the sign of the cross and then bowing to the crucifix.

During vacation the Cardinal observed the program of his daily life no less exactly than at Paris. He always rose early. At seven o'clock the church bells announced his Mass, at which many persons received Communion from his hands.

During his thanksgiving, poor people gathered along his return route to la Vergne, and there waited for him to come. Each in turn told his story, and Cardinal Richard listened patiently, while digging into his long red purse. Sometimes it became empty; one day, having nothing left, he gave his handkerchief to the last beggar. One morning a gypsy joined the ranks of the poor of the neighborhood. She asked nothing, but followed close after the Cardinal, who then held his hands behind his back and, still talking to those around him, dropped a few small coins as he walked along. The stranger understood and silently gathered up the manna.

The Cardinal's great-grandnephews asked for the honor of serving their granduncle's first breakfast. As to an indulgent grandfather, they brought him the coffee, the milk, the bread, but the one that presented the sugar to him always had it declined. Then the tireless Archbishop went to his own room to take care of his voluminous correspondence and to receive priests and sisters until lunch time. His room, which faced the south, was exceedingly warm during the summer mornings; when he came down to the dining room his zucchetto was wet through with perspiration.

During the meal he chatted gaily, asking questions about the persons he knew and their families. He ate with good appetite without much attention to what was set before him. After lunch he took a short walk with the family in the garden; along with his nephew, M. Charles Pellerin de la Vergne, he went to revisit the banks of the Sèvre where, as children, they used to romp and ride together. For these two old men it was an hour of real vacation and delightful friendliness in the setting of their happy memories. After his return to Paris, he wrote to his nephew: "We are two old boyhood friends; while we chat about present things, we give a large place to memories of the past. I think each of us is a little like old Horace, *laudator temporis acti.*"

The walk along the hillsides ended with a prayer at the Lourdes grotto. Then Cardinal Richard returned to his room and there continued to receive callers until evening. Various groups waited, in the reception room or on benches in the garden, to be presented to him. Some came, at times from far off, to seek advice, spiritual or material assistance. They all left happy, encouraged, and edified.

At about five o'clock the Cardinal went to the church for his visit to the Blessed Sacrament. From there he went to the cemetery, where he prayed a long time at the family vault which contained the remains of his father and mother. Stopping for a moment at the graves of the parish priests, he made a tour of the cemetery. As in the morning after his Mass, the people of the town waited for him along the road and presented their requests. The good Cardinal went into their homes, bringing help and comfort to the sick.

He also called at the parish rectory and at the school conducted by the Sisters of St. Gildas, where he said a few words to the children. On one such visit, he said: "If you should come to Paris you would see beautiful churches, beautiful monuments that would be new to you. But do not come, because you would there lose the most precious things you have, the simplicity of your faith and your good Christian habits."

The Cardinal wished to see in particular the la Vergne farmers, who generation after generation continued to live under the same roof. These visits he made immediately after the noon meal so that he might find the whole family together. He inquired about the old folks, about the young families to whom he had written at the time of their marriage, about the little children, to whom he gave holy pictures and medals. It was customary for the whole family to stand in silent attention as though they were in church. One day his rosary accidentally slipped from his pocket and fell to the floor. The mother of the family saw it but did not give it back to him at once because she wished first to touch it to various articles, as one might do with a relic of a saint.

In the evening, after dinner, the Cardinal spent an hour with his relatives, chatting in intimate friendly fashion. Seated in the armchair near the fireplace, he gently recalled the faces of the past and mingled them with the family gathered about him. "Before coming," he said, "I went to Issy to pray at the grave of my brother Louis. Were he still

alive, he would be a hundred years old today."
Then he spoke of Paris which he loved, of that
immense Paris where the works of charity were in-
creasing to counterbalance the evil. When speaking of Rome and of his first journeys there, which
he made by stagecoach, he adorned his accounts
with cheerful, picturesque details. While chatting
thus, he used to slip his pastoral ring along his
finger. Sometimes the ring fell on the floor, to the
delight of the children, who would then eagerly
hand the precious object back to him. Then perhaps they would take courage to ask him about "his
Paris horse." "So you want to know about my
horse," he would reply with a smile. "Well, my
dear children, his name is Coco, and he is not very
pretty." Often he spoke of the Church, so outraged
by the public authorities. "It is the work of freemasonry," he repeated; "you know its motto, 'Let
France perish, if only it ceases to be Christian.'"
And he insisted that good Christians, who are at
the same time good Frenchmen, should present a
living and active faith in opposition to the works
of the devil.

At about nine o'clock the Cardinal would have
the servants and the farm hands called for night
prayers. The doors of la Vergne were then thrown
wide open, and many persons of the town and of

the neighboring villages joined the members of the household to pray with the venerated Archbishop. The vestibule, the little parlor, often also the dining room, were filled. The Cardinal, kneeling in the middle of the parlor, recited the prayers aloud, and those present liked to hear him repeat this invocation to those who have gone before us to heaven: "Blessed souls, who have had the happiness to attain glory, obtain for me two things from our common God and Father, that I may never mortally offend Him and that He may take from me whatever displeases Him." As soon as the prayers were finished, the crowd quietly withdrew, so that the Cardinal was not aware of the large gathering that had been drawn by his presence.

Cardinal Richard liked to have the hospitable doors of la Vergne kept open to all comers. On the occasion of a family reunion, his nephews gave an evening party. The good Archbishop asked that the doors and windows should be left wide open, so that the good people of the neighborhood might be able to enter freely and see that in Christian families people could enjoy themselves without offending any proprieties. The people of the country readily profited by the permission. Only a few actually entered the house, but many looked on through the windows at this sight, which was altogether new for them. They were especially struck by the proper behavior of this evening party, and they went away edified.

During Cardinal Richard's short stays at la Vergne or l'Echasserie, visitors who came during the day were sometimes invited to remain for dinner. Some extra places were always set at the long table, at which the Cardinal presided with his genial cordiality.

In each parish where he owned some land, he generously aided the works of charity and particularly the Catholic schools. Thus he was fond of gathering about him the clergy of Boussay and those of the neighborhood to talk about the good that was to be done. After lunch, he conferred with each of them individually, from the venerable white-haired pastors to the young seminarians. The latter have kept the memory of the advice given them by the good Cardinal who, when going down to the old bower, would lean on their arm.

On Sunday the Cardinal was escorted in procession from the house to the church, where he presided at the High Mass. He always spoke a few words to the people. On one occasion the members of the church committee presented to His Eminence, in place of the blessed bread, an enormous cake. One year, at the time of the offertory, they carried to his throne a huge loaf of Savoy bread about three feet square. Cardinal Richard smiled and, since he could not keep this big present at his side during the Mass, said: "I thank you, my good friends; but please, for the moment, take it to the sacristy."

He spent Sunday in the midst of a considerable gathering of the clergy, among whom Father Caillé, who had been one of the Cardinal's fellow students, had a place of honor. In the rectory the good Archbishop found many reminders of former days and took notice of the least details of the gathering. One day, toward the end of the dinner, some word was brought to the curate of the parish, who replied in a low voice: "I will go presently." "Where, then, my son?" asked the Cardinal; "if it is some sick person who has sent for you, go at once." He was given the name of the sick person, an old man whom he knew, and he himself went to bring him a final consolation.

One Sunday evening the young men of the patronage presented an entertainment program. The Cardinal, who was present for the first portion, came away much pleased and amused.

In the Vendée the people awaited the coming of

the Cardinal with the same joy as did the people of Boussay. At l'Echasserie he continued his fatherly audiences and charitable visits. He saw all his farm tenants, solicitously inquiring about their needs, asking them about the events that had occurred in their homes since the previous year, and sharing their joys and sorrows. Before leaving, he invited them all to the Mass which he celebrated in his chapel for the deceased members of his family and those of his tenants. His great-grandnephew, Georges Couëspel du Mesnil, served his Mass as did the other boys of the family in the church of Boussay.

Again the Cardinal assembled his household in the chapel to recite the Angelus at noon. Patiently he waited until the voice of the small children finished the responses and he thanked their mothers for having taught them this prayer.

The neighborhood of the chapel at l'Echasserie offered a pleasant shade for a little gathering after lunch. Chatting cheerfully with those about him, the Cardinal was interested in watching the children at play in the garden. One day one of them, Georges Couëspel du Mesnil, became the owner of a little boat, the work of Clement, the gardener of l'Echasserie. At once the little group of cousins

199

worked out an elaborate project: at their next meeting together, the *Neptune* would be christened and launched. Each one was assigned an office for the occasion; the one named to be the sponsor obtained a provision of the requisite sugar-plums; his brother, chosen as the chief functionary, worked hard in preparing a discourse. On the appointed day, clothed in a cape of proper length, he delivered the speech as he stood before the decorated boat. Through the childlike phrases there rang so warm and Christian a patriotism that the amused parents joined in the festivity. The good Cardinal, taking the sheets of paper on which this address was written, read it and said: "My dear child, nothing is lacking from the exordium even to the peroration."

The parishes of la Bruffière and of St. Symphorian rejoiced to receive the good Archbishop. The people gathered in the church, eager to hear his words; but, as elsewhere, the poor and the sick were the object of his particular attention. At la Bruffière a former laborer of l'Echasserie had been afflicted with an attack of paralysis. The Cardinal went to visit him. The man's wife, upon seeing him enter their humble home, fell to her knees, and the paralytic, who was saying his beads, burst into tears. "Oh, my gentle master," he said. Cardinal Richard sat down beside the sick man and spoke words of spiritual comfort to him.

The people of the Vendée and of Nantes, deeply moved by the Cardinal's goodness of heart, retained a respectful fondness for him. A certain old man of Boussay used to tell his grandchildren, the Cardinal's great-grandnephews, that in his youth he went hunting with their great-granduncle. But he added: "Yes, indeed, my uncle went hunting with us. However, he carried his gun somewhat like a candle."

An old shell-fish merchant, who remembered the mother of the Cardinal, survived the latter. He had known five generations at la Vergne. For almost seventy years he came every week, bringing his shell-fish to the kitchen and measured them out in an old tin box. He would sit down and ask: "Monsieur Francis, I mean Monsignor, I mean His Eminence, is he still at Paris? We are the same age."

In 1901 the Cardinal obtained permission from the Bishop of Luçon to confirm the children of St. Symphorian, among whom were three of his own great-grandnephews. The occasion was a great feast day for the little town.

The Cardinal did not take more than one week of vacation. Even those few days were, like his ordinary life, filled with good works, as we have seen. Still he cherished the hours of leisure. He wrote:

I preserve a happy recollection of those moments we passed together in our family gathering. I can never remain long with you, but as the years go on, the duties and labors also increase and I feel the need of making a good use of the time that Providence grants me. Although the will of the good God keeps me at a distance, I seem to love you the more. When I baptized your third baby, I thanked the good God. . . . I may confess that I could not keep from smiling when writing the venerable title of "Grandpapa" as I recalled our memories of the days when you were the youngest of the band of big boys of that far-off time. Then I think of the blessings that the good God has continued to bestow on our family for more than half a century, preserving its traditions of Christian living through the vicissitudes inseparable from the present life, and I feel my soul filled with gratitude. . . . Like all who live here below, we have had our joys and our griefs, but the good God has given us the grace, as the Church says in her prayers, that, "amid the vanities of the world, our hearts may be fixed there, where the true joys are."

Outside his vacations the Cardinal, so far as his pastoral duties permitted, returned to his family to bless their marriages and to baptize their children. On these occasions his visits were very short.

It is understood, of course, that I shall arrive without any beating of drums or blowing of trumpets. You will fix the hour of the baptism, at whatever time suits you best, on Thursday the 14th. I have not time to write to

Albert or to Margaret or even to Mlle Yvonne. Her grand-mother Antonie will see to it that she learns that her great-granduncle is most happy to baptize her.

The good Archbishop visited his old home country incognito. To do so was no easy matter, even when he removed the tassel of his hat, so as to pass less noticed. One day when he was thus slowly passing through the church of St. Peter at Nantes, the old sexton, whose life was spent almost entirely within the walls of his cathedral, hastened his step to join the visitor, whom he did not at first recognize. But as he came closer, he cried out with joy: "Oh, my Cardinal!"

Another day the secret of his coming to Boussay had been carefully kept. But a boy perceived at a distance, on the road from la Bruffière, a carriage that he seemed to recognize. Then he met M. de la Vergne, who appeared to be waiting for someone. Now the young miller had no longer any doubt. "Oh, Monsieur! It is Monseigneur, is it not? The people must prepare a bonfire at once." Then calling the men who were at work nearby, he said to them: "Quick, lads. The Cardinal will be here in a few minutes." Hurriedly the wood was heaped up in the middle of the square in front of the church. Meanwhile the Cardinal was told by his nephew: "They have seen you, Uncle." But he was not at all annoyed or displeased, and told his coachman: "Drive slowly to give these good children time to finish their preparations."

The Cardinal not only took part in the joyous events of the family; when sorrow came to any of its members, he lavished on them the marks of his fatherly attachment. The sick received affectionate encouragement from him, and he himself came to the bedside of the dying to give them some final comfort.

He wrote to a friend as follows:

I greatly appreciate your kind remembrance on the occasion of the death of Madame de Couëssin. I was able to see her, to bid her farewell, and to bless her for the last time, before she left us. I was much consoled at the Christian dispositions with which she faced the approach of death; and I thank God for giving her this grace of a good death. She had no illusions about her condition and peacefully resigned herself into the hands of God. Pray with us, my dear brother, for this good deceased woman, and pray also for the husband and the five children that she left in this world.

The Cardinal did not have the consolation of seeing thus at the last hour his beloved nephew Charles, to whose son he wrote: "At my last visit to Nantes your father and I talked together more intimately than ever, like travelers who are bidding each other good-bye. We felt that life's journey was nearing its end for us. . . . Only in Christian families can you find real affection, since this love does not end with this life."

For three years more Cardinal Richard brought the comfort of his presence to la Vergne and l'Echasserie. He pleaded the grief of the persecutions to decline any solemn receptions, but his bearing remained charitably open to all.

This was especially understood by those who were united to him by ties of blood and by those also who saw him in the intimacy of these family gatherings, surrounded like a patriarch by four generations and sharing his delicate attentions with them all.

The Cardinal was on the point of setting out from Paris in 1903 when he became anxious for the health of his valet Joseph. He wrote as follows to his nephew Albert:

By this time you have my telegram of this morning, in which I sent you word that I could not leave today on account of the serious condition of my poor Joseph. He has now been paralyzed for about eighteen months. Recently he became somewhat weaker, and now suddenly his condition has become much worse. This morning he asked me to give him the last sacraments, which I did at ten o'clock. You know that Joseph was very devout. We are now taking him to the Brothers of St. John of God, where he will undergo an operation. Joseph is seventy-six years old; an operation at that age is always serious. I find comfort in having given him Viaticum and extreme unction this morning. You understand, my dear Albert, that I cannot abandon this good Joseph, who has served me so devoutly for more than thirty years.

The next day Cardinal Richard announced: "Our good Joseph died about midnight. His end came quietly. The operation, which the doctors considered urgent, was performed yesterday evening.

"I must now give up my journey to Boussay and l'Echasserie. I shall not have enough time before the retreat. This is a sacrifice which the good God asks of me. I pray Him to bless us all the more for this sacrifice."

A few weeks later the Cardinal was able to make the journey. "My dear children," he said when he reached la Vergne, "what a sacrifice the good God asked of our good Pius X in not permitting him to see his native country any more!" Though not realizing the fact, the holy prelate was also making a farewell visit to the country of his childhood.

In August of the following year he accepted an invitation to bless four bells in the church of la Bruffière. On the largest of them was engraved the Cardinal's motto. All of them carried this inscription: "I was blessed on August 23 of the year of grace 1904 by His Eminence Cardinal Richard, Archbishop of Paris." But, owing to a sore leg, he was unable to go.

Shortly afterward he again planned to visit his homeland. But the doctors again advised against the journey. At once he wrote to the family not to postpone the supplying of the baptism ceremonies for another little niece. He wrote:

I shall be with you in spirit all day. Tomorrow I will say Mass for the dear little Annick Marie Frances, asking the good God that she may ever preserve the grace of her baptism; and I will embrace all of you in that same intention: father, mother, brothers, and sisters, without forgetting the good grandmothers. I shall thus be near you by prayer during that glorious day. As you say in your letter, we will not forget our dear parents, who have gone to God before us. The great strength and joy of Christian families is the knowledge that, with the grace of God, we shall meet in His holy paradise.

The Cardinal never again saw his native country. But he was always happy to receive visits from members of his family. His weekly letters to them are filled with a solicitous interest in the education of the children, plans for the future, the happiness of each of them. He expressed his concern about the health of one of his nephews, who had been injured by a fall from a horse. To help his memory, the venerable granduncle made a list of the names of his numerous great-grandnephews, with the date of their birth. He used to read over this family litany that he might speak to the good God about each one in particular.

One of these children, Ernest de Kerdudal, came to Paris to the School of St. Genevieve, as did also one of his cousins, Henry Le Lièvre de la Touche. The Cardinal had them visit him on their holidays. He sent his carriage for them and received them at his table. To help them spend the day pleasantly, he placed them in the charge of one of his immediate entourage and gave orders that they were to enjoy something good in the nearest pastry-shop at four o'clock. At dinner in the evening the Cardinal dispensed with the usual table reading. Both of these boys died on the battlefield during the World War.

The Cardinal liked to give pleasure to all. One of his great-grandnieces asked his blessing for some undertaking about which he was not well enough informed. But he thought he ought not grant this favor at once without knowing more about the matter. He wrote to her as follows:

I do not wish you to think of your uncle's letter merely as a refusal. So the thought came to me to present you with my volume, *Les Saints de l'Eglise de Nantes*. I am

208

going to have a copy bound especially for you and will send it to you in the course of the week. I bless you together with your brothers and sisters, asking the good God to give you the grace to be always the comfort and joy of your excellent parents.

These children's mother had asked the Cardinal to procure for her a certain relic, which, however, he was unable to obtain. In his boundless kindness he wished to lessen her disappointment. He had a little silver medallion containing a piece of the true cross and always wore this heirloom, as his mother herself had done. Now he deprived himself of it and gave it to his niece.

Three months before the Cardinal's death, one of his nieces at la Vergne was expecting the birth of a tenth child. Several times the Archbishop said to the members of his household: "If you will be so kind, we will recite this decade of the Rosary for my niece, who will soon have another child, the tenth." When he was informed of the arrival in this world of his thirty-fourth great-grandniece, he telegraphed: "I bless the little protégée of Our Lady of the Rosary and her mother." A few days later he sent to this latest niece a gold medal, as he had done for her many brothers and sisters and cousins. After his death one of his vicars general, when he came to la Vergne, recalling the many decades of the Rosary which His Eminence had recited for this intention, said: "Now show me the tenth."

To the end of his life, Cardinal Richard preserved his fondness for the priests whom he had known at Nantes and in the neighborhood. He kept up a continual correspondence with them and encouraged their good works. Father Durand, pastor of Boussay, having died, the Cardinal was eager to make the acquaintance of his successor, Father Maussion, who went to Paris to call on him. On the day announced for the visit, the Archbishop, in his eagerness to know the new pastor, came downstairs twice to ask: "Has the pastor of Boussay arrived?"

The poor, so beloved by the Cardinal, did not suffer by his absence. Through the intermediary of two of his nephews, at the beginning of each winter he had clothing distributed among them and also firewood that had been gathered on his lands. Throughout the year the bakeries had an open account for the needy families.

Toward the afflicted, the good Cardinal became the cashier of the good God. Every sort of suffering, whether of body or soul, found in him relief and comfort.

CHAPTER XV

The Cardinal's Last Years

THE Cardinal, feeling himself growing old and
not wishing to be an obstacle to the accomplishment of good, twice offered his resignation to
Leo XIII at his annual visits to Rome. But the
Pope declined to accept the resignation and obliged
him to remain at his post; and the Cardinal obeyed.

The Holy Father had a deep esteem for the virtues of Cardinal Richard. In 1899 the Cardinal was
in Rome for the feast of St. Francis de Sales (January 29). The Pope, wishing to join in the good
wishes extended to him, sent him his blessing and
some flowers from the Vatican Garden.

Somewhat later a perfect harmony of views, a
oneness of aspirations, and the same supernatural
serenity in the midst of the trials of the Church,
daily strengthened the bonds of veneration that
united Cardinal Richard to Pius X.

Notwithstanding his advanced age and the heavy

burdens of his office, Cardinal Richard preserved a wonderful clearness of mind and continued to administer his vast diocese amid the great difficulties that afflicted the Church of France. He never thought of seeking repose. To the very end of his life, his labor was interrupted only by prayer. From time to time his infirmities obliged him to remain in bed. Even then he continued to write letters and to attend to official business, his correspondence and documents at his side within reach. Sometimes, when absorbed in his work, he used the red satin bedspread as a pen-wiper.

In his government of the diocese he considered himself solely responsible; this was a matter of conscience with him. For almost all questions that he had to examine, he promptly found the principle of their solution in canon law and theology. But, to assure himself that he was not mistaken, he would go to his library, take from a shelf the volume where the question was treated, and open it, saying: "It is to the right, or to the left, at such a part of the page." Everything, to the smallest details, passed through his hands. Said Father Icard, the superior of St. Sulpice: "Of all the bishops of France, Cardinal Richard is the one who is best acquainted with the tasks of his office."

The Cardinal's last years were greatly saddened

by consequences of the law of separation. From the outset he saw plainly what was being prepared. "What they wish," he said, "is to laicize the Church, to destroy religion. This is the plan pursued by the antichristian sects." By this expression he was referring to freemasonry.

The Cardinal astounded the lawyers and the canonists by his knowledge. After prolonged discussions, he always ended by saying: "If the law is not changed, we cannot accept it, because it is a lay constitution of the Church of France."

On January 31, 1906, the Catholics of the Madeleine interfered to prevent the inventory. The pastor, Father Chesnelong, called on the Cardinal to acquaint him with what was happening. The Cardinal was then confined to bed. Receiving Father Chesnelong at his bedside, he said to him: "By protesting as you have done, by acting in conformity with the instructions of your archbishop, you have done your duty. The faithful, by protesting as they have done, have likewise done their duty. God be praised!"

After the Catholics' resistance to the pillage of two churches in Paris, some persons came to the Cardinal and begged him to intervene to put an end to the resistance. "I cannot blame the Catholics," he said, "for defending their churches. On the contrary, I ought to congratulate them for their zeal, while recommending calmness and obedience to their bishop."

Cardinal Richard followed all the movements of the enemy like an experienced commander; not for a moment was he fooled, not for a moment did he deviate from the line he had marked out. He then appeared as the real head of the Church of France, he who, in his humility, had never consented to assume that role. The bishops, in their meetings, recognized him as such. All bowed before his lofty wisdom and, on the day of his obsequies, Cardinal Lecot said: "He was the guide of the French episcopate, not merely by the brilliance of his incomparable virtues, but also by that clear vision which came from his holiness, and by that light which came to him from on high, to lead him in the midst of the obscurity of the present hour."

As the years passed, the Cardinal became more and more concerned over the question of his successor. He often said: "I ask the good God that I may die at the moment that will be the most favorable for the appointment of my successor and the greatest good of the diocese." He considered resigning so as to facilitate this appointment for the Holy Father. Events did in fact permit him to make the choice himself, as Pius X invited him to do in November, 1905, through the intermediary of Bishop Fages.

In January, 1906, he profited by the liberty which the law of separation gave him, to choose a coadjutor. This he did during the novena of St. Genevieve, the patron saint of Paris, to whom he had a great devotion. He prayed to her to guide him in this choice. He spoke of the matter to Bishop Jourdan de la Passardière, who favored the Cardinal's choice of Bishop Amette of Bayeux. The Cardinal then sought counsel from the superior general of St. Sulpice, who was commissioned to approach Bishop Amette on the question. The latter at first refused, but then agreed to leave the matter in the hands of the Holy Father, who confirmed Cardinal Richard's choice. This decision gave the Archbishop a feeling of security for the future of the Church of Paris. Presently he began little by little to withdraw from external activities and lived more in recollection and prayer, though without ceasing to be interested in the affairs of the diocese.

The persecution was becoming more brutal. The Nuncio's secretary, Monsignor Montagnini, had been arrested and conducted to the Italian border. The Archbishop of Paris, like all his fellow bish-

215

ops, had received notice that he must vacate his residence.

On the evening of December 14, 1906, the report spread that Cardinal Richard would be expelled the next day. Several hundred persons promptly gathered at his residence. Shortly before two o'clock in the afternoon an unknown person presented himself and asked to speak to the Archbishop of Paris. This caller was the police commissioner for the Champs-Elysées district.

Archbishop Amette at once went to the Cardinal, who had been ailing for some time past. From his bed he had already dictated the writing down of the arrangements that should be made. Ready for any eventuality, he had left his bed that morning and at the time was in his study, seated at his desk where he had written so many letters and drawn up so many plans. Archbishop Amette was standing at the Cardinal's right, the vicars general and the other officers of the diocesan administration were grouped about the large desk. M. Paul Lerolle, the Paris deputy, was present. The police commissioner was then introduced. The Cardinal, in accordance with his habitual courtesy, instinctively stood up, but Archbishop Amette urged him to remain seated to receive such a communication. The commissioner advanced to the middle of the circle and there the representative of force, visibly upset, his legs trembling, greeted this old unarmed man who looked at him without harshness. "By the letter of the prefect," he said, "Your Eminence has been notified that after December 12, you can no longer occupy the residence which has heretofore been placed at your disposal by the state. As the extension of the time has now expired, the prefect of police instructs me . . . in due legal form, to have the occupied property vacated."

This notification, haltingly made, with an evident concern to safeguard the proprieties, was followed by an agonizing silence which the Cardinal himself broke. Looking steadily at the police commissioner, he said: "You come to put me out. I will leave only under constraint. I protest against the violation of the rights and the freedom of the Church." He then added: "I wish to know whether you consider the legal notification which you have just delivered as a constraint." When his question had been answered in the affirmative, he said: "I will leave Monday."

As he departed, the commissioner could see in the courtyard the crowd that had assembled there. But they did not leave, thinking that the commissioner was going to return. At four o'clock the Cardinal asked Archbishop Amette to express his

217

thanks to these devoted people and to bless them in his name.

Early in the afternoon of Monday, December 17, a crowd again filled the courtyard. The clergy came into the vestibule and the reception rooms of the ground floor. Several Catholic notables were brought to the waiting room on the next floor, where the members of the diocesan administration were gathered, who were now joined by Bishop Gibier of Versailles.

The Cardinal had remained in his private rooms, busy with attending to several affairs and in classifying his papers in his study. At half-past one, he was interrupted and was told that everything was ready for his departure.

He arose at once, warmly thanked Bishop Gibier and the valiant Catholics who were there about him. Then, with the help of some priests, painfully he went down the great stairs, which had so often led him from his study to the chapel. When he reached the foot of the stairs and saw there a large number of his clergy, he decided once more in their presence to protest against the violation of the rights and liberties of the Church.

When he appeared at the head of the front steps, the crowd, which just before had been singing the Credo, acclaimed their Archbishop. Deeply moved at sight of this multitude, whose presence he had been unaware of, he pronounced in a strong voice the words of the episcopal blessing over the kneeling throng. Then he entered the carriage with Archbishop Amette and Bishop Fages.

The carriage started out, but with unaccustomed slowness. In a moment the horse was unharnessed and its place taken by a group of young men. A procession of 15,000 persons formed the impromptu escort. Shouts of, "Liberty! Long live the Cardinal! Long live Pius X!" were followed by the singing of the Credo and of the *Parce Domine*. The journey was not longer than a third of a mile, but it took an hour, the Cardinal continually blessing the crowd that pressed about him.

A fearless Catholic, Baron Cochin, had offered Cardinal Richard asylum in his palace on rue de Babylone. There it was that the long procession halted. Into the courtyard the young men drew the carriage, to the very steps of the house. Only then did the two archbishops note that the horse had disappeared and they now understood why the carriage had moved along in so unusual a manner. The Cardinal extended his hands over the kneeling throng, then entered the apartments which had been prepared for him by Baron and Baroness Cochin.

Eager to receive their Archbishop's blessing, several young men had invaded the garden. They had a glimpse of the Cardinal seated near a large window and for more than an hour they passed before him. Meanwhile Archbishop Amette invited the crowd to go to the church of St. Francis Xavier. At the Benediction of the Blessed Sacrament, after singing the prayer for the Pope, he intoned, *Pro pontifice nostro Francisco.* The crowd present responded enthusiastically and asked God not to deliver their Archbishop into the hands of his enemies.

At five o'clock that evening, silence descended upon the palace on rue de Babylone. After being assured that their guest lacked nothing, the Baron and the Baroness withdrew with delicate consideration. The Cardinal was advised to rest a little. "I will do so," he said, "by saying my breviary." At dinner that evening the Cardinal had at table with him those who habitually ate with him. Following his daily custom, they recited the Rosary in common.

A private chapel had been arranged in a little parlor, where Cardinal Richard could go directly from his apartment. Care had been taken that the venerable prelate might enjoy the best possible comfort and quiet. Starting the next day, he was able to celebrate Mass in the improvised chapel. The presence of the Blessed Sacrament was a consolation for him.

At once he set to work. He expressed his thanks to the people who had shown so filial a devotion to him, extending his thanks personally to all those he could reach. In spite of such a confusion and the scattering of the material needed for his daily work, the Cardinal wished that nothing should be neglected, whether it concerned the diocesan administration or the defense of the interests of the Church of France.

However kind and generous the hospitality of Baron and Baroness Cochin, the Cardinal did not wish to impose upon that charity. A house was found on rue de Bourgogne, that was then unoccupied. Thither he had the innumerable documents of the archdiocese carried by his seminarians. This task lasted three days.

Apart from his books and some articles of piety, Cardinal Richard no longer had for his use anything of his own at the time of his expulsion from the archiepiscopal residence. Some charitable gifts enabled him to replace the modest furniture of his room: a bed, a few chairs, and the desk on which he wrote his last letters.

The installation on rue de Bourgogne could not

be favorable to a shattered health. The Cardinal himself had foreseen the weakening of his strength and desired that his room should be close to the chapel so that he might follow Mass from his bed. Pope Pius X had authorized him to celebrate Mass sitting down during the part of the Mass before the Canon. But he rarely made use of this privilege.

No longer able to go to Rome, he sent a confidential messenger to express his filial sentiments to the Pope. Upon leaving an audience, at which he had set forth to the Holy Father a request of Cardinal Richard, this envoy wrote: "The Pope listened attentively to the reading of Your Eminence's whole letter. Then he took it and, making over it a big sign of the cross, he said to me: 'Write to the Cardinal that I am deeply touched by his sentiments in my regard. . . . My wish is that he may live longer than I.' The Holy Father several times repeated these words, that Your Eminence must live after him."

To Cardinal Richard's vicars general, the Holy Father said: "I think of the Cardinal of Paris not merely every day, but several times a day. Tell him that the Pope orders him to live and forbids him to die. To the Cardinal, for whom I have so great affection and veneration, you will carry the heart of the Pope." These testimonies of the Holy Father's friendship rejoiced the heart of the old Archbishop, but at the same time tested his humility. He said: "I do not know what I have done, that the Pope treats me thus."

However, the years were adding to his physical ailments. At times his sufferings forced a faint sigh, but they never disturbed his serenity, which came from his complete abandonment to divine Providence.

In December, 1904, the hernia, from which he had been suffering for a long time, became aggravated. His two physicians called a celebrated specialist, Dr. Berger, in consultation. After an examination of the patient, all three withdrew to another room. Presently Dr. Berger returned and said: "Your Eminence, our opinion is that we should not operate for the hernia from which you have been suffering several years. At your age, the tissues are stretched and, when we would sew them, they might easily tear loose along the suture. You had better remain as you are." "That is also my opinion," the Cardinal replied. "It is what I said to myself during your consultation. You see, I am the son of a doctor. And besides, according to the Gospel, no one can sew a piece of new cloth on an old garment, because then the old will be rent."

At about this time one of his relatives died at

Nantes at the age of 104 years. When someone expressed to the Cardinal the wish that he might live to that age, he replied: "Like St. Martin, 'I do not refuse the labor,' but all I wish is to do the will of God." For three or four years past he had been repeating: "This is my last year." Now he felt his end approaching and said to his priests in his letter of August 15, 1907: "We ask you to be mindful of your old Archbishop when God calls him to Himself."

The Cardinal no longer had at his disposal a large house for the many gatherings. The diocesan offices occupied the greater part of the house on rue de Bourgogne. On the second floor, facing the street, was the Archbishop's private apartment consisting of two rooms near his chapel: a little sitting room and a bedroom. For the meeting of the bishops on January 15, 1907, he accepted the gracious offer of the Count de Franqueville, a member of the Institute, who placed at the Cardinal's disposal the château of la Muette. To receive the New Year's greetings of his clergy in 1908, he used the Condé palace, placed at his disposal for the occasion.

Three days later he saw pass before him the delegations of the principal works of charity, about two thousand persons. He seemed to be reviewing for the last time the forces of good of his great diocese and to be handing them over to his coadjutor.

On January 15 he crowned his long episcopate of thirty-three years by an act worthy of the great bishops of the Middle Ages. He went to the Bon Secours hospice to receive the sisters of the Hôtel Dieu, driven out by the law of separation, from the very place which sixteen centuries earlier a bishop of Paris, St. Landry, had opened to their charity.

No one who witnessed this scene will forget that august old man, suffering from pains in his legs, carried in an armchair by the doctors of the hospital. Like the ninety-year-old St. John, in the midst of the assembled faithful, with his blessing and his smile and his fatherly words he consoled and encouraged the sisters, the weeping patients, and their friends. Thus it was that in the house of the poor, of the little ones, of the suffering, who had ever been the object of his concern and solicitude, he made his last appearance before the people of Paris.

Four days later, Monsignor Odelin, his chief vicar, said to him: "Your Eminence, your going to the Bon Secours last Wednesday was a sort of youthful escapade; was it not imprudent?" "Oh no," he answered. "You see, I am no longer any good from the waist down; but I am still sound above. I have not good legs any more, but I still have a good head."

That was Sunday, January 19. On Tuesday he was busily occupied. As usual, and now for the last time, he presided at the meeting of the archiepiscopal council and received several callers. The next day he celebrated Mass for the last time, assisted by Father Lefebvre. The venerable invalid did not wish to interrupt his occupations.

On Thursday evening he was aware of the gravity of his condition and repeatedly said that the end of his life was at hand. Speaking to his confessor about a venerable bishop who had just died rather suddenly, he said: "I shall go like that; I am going to die in two or three days." He asked for the sacrament of extreme unction. But, upon the advice of the attending physicians, he waited with docility.

Sunday evening his condition suddenly became worse. The fever returned, and he had two fainting spells. The doctors declared that the congestion had reached the lungs and that his condition was serious. Archbishop Amette proposed to him that he receive extreme unction. "No," he replied; "this morning the doctors did not advise it; I am not sick

226

enough." Dr. Le Bec then told him that, since the
morning, his condition had become much worse
and that he would do well to do that evening what
he had wished to do that morning. "Very well,"
said the Cardinal; "I wish to see my confessor."
He made his confession and said: "Give me ten
minutes to prepare myself." At the end of a quarter of an hour, he said: "I am ready. Archbishop
Amette and those gentlemen may come in." In
spite of the late hour, all the diocesan officials had
been notified. At nine o'clock they gathered about
their venerated father while Archbishop Amette
gave him extreme unction. He received this sacrament with perfect clearness of mind and serenity,
answering the prayers and making the signs of the
cross at the blessings of the Church.

In the name of the clergy and faithful of Paris,
Archbishop Amette thanked the holy Cardinal for
all the good he had done during his long ministry and asked his fatherly blessing for all. In a
voice already broken and gasping but distinctly
heard by all those present, the venerable prelate
said: "I abandon myself entirely to the divine will.
I can scarcely speak any longer, but I still have
strength to bless you with all my heart. I bless this
whole beloved diocese, the priests, the religious

communities, the faithful, and my dear coadjutor; and I thank God for having given him to me for the close of my life."

Raising his feeble hands, he blessed those present. Then he continued: "And now I entrust this beloved Church of Paris to the keeping of the Blessed Virgin; I confide it to the Sacred Heart of Jesus, to His supreme rule and His mercy; again I bless it and especially its good priests, whom I love, it seems to me, more and more. Let them remember me and pray for me." A second time he made the sign of the cross and pronounced the words of blessing over all present, without forgetting the servants.

The next day he decided to resume his customary practices of piety. He asked for his missal that he might follow the Mass celebrated in the chapel beside his bedroom, and he even tried to read his breviary until the end of the day. He sent for Father Thomas to go over with him some details of his will and to attend to some final business affairs.

About noon the Holy Father, informed of the Cardinal's condition, sent him his apostolic blessing, with an assurance of his prayers and of his affection. The venerable Cardinal had the message placed before his eyes, near the crucifix. In the evening he spoke again of this kindness of the Pope.

But that same evening the doctors observed that his life was gradually slipping away.

Father Garriguet, His Eminence's confessor, who had assisted him from the outset of this illness, spent the night at his bedside together with some of the Archbishop's household. They heard him repeat some invocations from the psalms and from the litany of the Blessed Virgin. At half-past four in the morning he said: "I cannot see my crucifix or my beads any longer, yet I am still holding them." At five o'clock Archbishop Amette recited the prayers for those in their last agony. The Cardinal himself made all the responses, and said: "I am not so sick, I am going to get up and say my prayers on my knees." While his breathing was growing weaker, two Masses were said in the adjoining chapel. At the end of the second Mass, the beautiful soul of the holy Archbishop left this world and returned to its Maker.

———————

The Pope, upon receiving the sad news, telegraphed at once: "The Holy Father, deeply afflicted by the sad news of the death of the venerable and beloved Cardinal Richard, a model of priestly life and a faithful shepherd, shares in the mourning of the Church of France."

Index

INDEX

INDEX

Richard, Francis (Bishop of Belley), 103-18
canonization of the Curé of Ars, 110
coat of arms of, 97
confirmation circuit, 108
consecration of, 95, 101 f.
illnesses of, 115 f.
the *Messager du Dimanche* founded by, 107
pilgrimages, 112 f.
recitation of the breviary, 106
at Rome, 110, 117
zeal of, 105 ff.

Richard, Francis (Cardinal), 141-229
Admiral Avellane received by, 179
Alfonso XIII received by, 180
amiability of, 181
annual visits to Rome, 148
antireligious laws, 176 f.
beatifications and canonizations, 169
at Belley, 184
Bishop Amette becomes coadjutor of, 215
at Boussay, 146
calls on Czar Nicholas II, 179
Chancellor of the Catholic Institute, 153
charity of, 150, 184 f., 191, 210
confirmation of a dying ragpicker, 182 f.
daily meditation, 151
daily Scripture reading, 151
dealings with the government, 173-78
death of, 229
death of his valet Joseph, 206
defense of church property, 213
diocesan missioners founded by, 163
diocesan works of charity, 167 f.

Richard, Francis (Card.) *(cont.)*
exact knowledge of his diocese, 162 f.
expelled from his residence, 216 ff.
fondness for Notre Dame Cathedral, 158
foreign missions, 168
golden jubilee of his priesthood, 148 f.
guest of Baron Cochin, 221
hernia, 223
hour of rising, 151
illnesses of, 145, 156, 175, 186, 212, 223
labors of, 151-87
last Mass of, 226
last years of, 211-29
letters: from Bishop Touchet, 156; from Leo XIII, 157; to Combes, 177; to Leo XIII, 156; to the President of France, 165; to Waldeck-Rousseau, 155 f.
at Lourdes, 145
modernism, 170
Montmartre Basilica, 159-61
moves from his residence, 218 f.
new churches in Paris, 162
offers his resignation, 211
Paris Exposition (1900), 173
particular examen of conscience, 151
persecution of the Church by the government, 175 ff.
pilgrimages, 187
prayer, 151 f.
privileged to celebrate Mass sitting down, 222
the ragpickers of Paris, 182
receives extreme unction, 226 f.
reception of the red zucchetto, 142 f.
religious communities, 154 f.
requests for alms, 183

233

INDEX

235

CARMELITE MONASTERY
Beckley Hill
Barre, Vt., 05641

DATE BORROWED